CANDY
KINGPIN

To: Bria
Always Big Love
from me to you.
May my story inspire
and encourage you
to lean on your faith
and live life to the
fullest!

Love to life

Rahf

Other books by Rahfeal Gordon

Skyscraper: Going Beyond Your Limits to Reach Your Greatness

Leading Without Limits: How to Become a Global Leader

Opulence: Mastering Your Finances, Power, and Mindset

CANDY KINGPIN

A MEMOIR

RAHFEAL C. GORDON

Madison **+** Park

A Global Branding Agency

Madison + Park
A Global Branding Agency
3017 Bolling Way NE Suite 259
Atlanta, Georgia 30305

Phone: +01 (678) 208-3571
info@madpar.com
www.MadPar.com

@madisonparkagency

3nd Edition. Previous title: *One23: A Memoir of RahGor*

ISBN: 978-1-7346316-6-1 (hardcover)
ISBN: 978-1-7346316-7-8 (softcover)

Because of the dynamic nature of the Internet, any web addresses or
links contained in this book may have changed since publication and
may no longer be valid. The views expressed in this work are solely those
of the author and do not necessarily reflect the views of the publisher,
and the publisher hereby disclaims any responsibility for them.

Cover Photography by Baa-ith Nurri-Deen

Book Design by DesignForBooks.com

DEDICATION

This book is dedicated to every person in my global village.
Thank you for helping me find my way during my journey to
make a way for others.

+

This book is also dedicated to every person that
is trying to find their way.
Just remain focus and stay persistent.
Your time is coming.
Prepare for it.

CONTENTS

"To think health when surrounded by the appearance of disease, or to think riches when the midst of appearance of poverty, requires power; but he who acquires this power becomes a MASTER MIND. He can conquer fate; he can have what he wants."

—WALLACE D. WATTLES

1

FLASHBACK
WHEN I WAS YOUNG

I n the beginning, from what I can remember, my life was wonderful. I was the oldest of four boys, and we lived with my parents on Weequahic Avenue in Newark, New Jersey. My neighborhood was known as the Weequahic section.

As a young boy, I attended Maple Avenue School, otherwise known as "Little Maple," from kindergarten to third grade. I made honor roll every cycle, and I remember receiving high-fives from my father when he read my report card. My mother would be so proud and say, *"That's right! My Rah is smart."*

Those proud moments of my parents made me so happy. The expressions on their faces motivated me to maintain good grades and achieve greater success in school. After I graduated from "Little Maple," I was supposed to attend "Big Maple" to start fourth grade. Instead, my family moved to South 10th Street off South Orange Avenue in Newark before the start of the school year, and I attended a different school. Times were still good for us as a family because no matter where we moved, we were all still together.

While living on South 10th Street, my brothers and I were known as the Gordon Boys. We were always having fun together on our block, and since there were four of us, we didn't really have too many other friends. At the same time, the few friends we did have loved hanging out with us. We weren't destructive kids, but some people may still beg to differ. As young boys, we played traditional games such as freeze tag, hide-and-go seek, manhunt, wallzy, and the hood favorite game with bottle tops called "tops." Those were the days! When we were allowed to sit on the porch, my father or mother would give me a dollar to buy everyone ice pops, sunflower seeds, and dime juices.

As young boys, we played traditional games such as freeze tag, hide-and-go seek, manhunt, wallzy, and the hood favorite game with bottle tops called "tops." Those were the days!

My mother and father were the best parents for my brothers and me. My mother cooked delicious meals for us every night, and on Fridays, my father would take our family to Pizza Hut in Jersey City. We would be so excited that once we finished eating at Pizza Hut, we would eagerly talk about what we would order the next time we came.

My grandfather owned an auto body shop in West New York that is located in the state of New Jersey, and my father worked for him. On weekends, my father would take us to the shop to see Grandpa and all our Hispanic friends. It seemed as if we were the only black kids in the area. I remember a funny incident where we thought that one of the fellas was African American, and he burst out speaking Spanish. It was in West New York that we experienced a culture other than our own.

We made some of the best friends in West New York. My father would visit the park on his lunch break and play basketball with me. All my friends would watch in amazement while cheering me on to beat him. It was as if I represented the youth, and the playground was our territory. No adult, not even my father, was allowed to come in and win any of the games we played.

My father would visit the park on his lunch break and play basketball with me.

While Janvier and I played basketball, Alfonso and Isaiah enjoyed gymnastics. They would draw huge crowds of people who watched in amazement as they did 50 back flips in succession. Likewise, people would crowd around Janvier and me just to see us beat everyone on the court. It was the spark of the Gordon Boys making their name in a West New York neighborhood that was only theirs for the weekend.

During the summer, my father would take trips after work to Chinatown and buy $200 worth of fireworks for the block. Our friends back in Newark would ask, *"When is your father bringing home firecrackers?"* It was something everyone anticipated. Whenever he returned with firecrackers, he wouldn't let anyone know until a day later.

For example, I remember one occasion where my father woke me up at 6:00 a.m. to go with him to work on a Saturday. At the same time, my mother was diligently preparing us breakfast. She said, *"Look at my two men getting ready for work."* When we finished breakfast and headed to the car, my mother looked out the window and said, *"Be good and I love you Rah."* I yelled back that I loved her too. My father laughed and led me to the trunk. When he opened it, I saw all the fireworks. He removed an M-80 firecracker and lit it with his morning cigarette. Once it exploded at about 6:45 a.m., the entire neighborhood knew that Mr. Gordon had firecrackers.

Life was golden for my brothers and me. We would see family members on holidays, birthdays, social gathers, cookouts, and school functions. We were blessed to have two sets of grandparents to interact with and love. It was these moments that kept me smiling. But hard times were on the horizon, and one may wonder what went wrong.

2

MOMENT
OF CLARITY

As I write these memories of my life, it hurts me to know that I always had the answer to a problem that could have been solved with constant love, attention, and affection.

The problems for my family slowly developed. I remember my father would sometimes come home late from work, and my mother would worry about his whereabouts. Now, this could have always been an issue, but at my age, I didn't pay it any attention. Likewise, during some weekends, my parents couldn't afford a babysitter, so I would have to watch my brothers while they went to work. It was difficult because at times we didn't have any food in the house.

I can recall a time when we were so hungry that I went into the refrigerator and found a roll of biscuits. We were not allowed to touch the oven, so we started thinking creatively on how to prepare the biscuits. I thought about heat sources and the alternatives available that could substitute as an oven. I debated using the radiator, but when I inspected it further, it was too rusty. Then I considered a lamp that had no shade, and I began placing raw biscuits on the light bulb. I don't need to share with you the result of this experiment. As you laugh at my strategy, you are not

*A*t one of my birthday parties, my intoxicated father arrived unexpectedly. In front of all my friends and brothers, he beat me.

alone. My brothers still crack jokes about my failed attempt to cook those biscuits.

Around this time living on South 10th Street, there was increased tension between my parents which I could not understand. My mother and father would increasingly argue. My father would come home inebriated and high after work. My mother would start to disappear when my father came home which my brothers and I did not like. We had this fear about our father that was just was getting stronger and stronger. How could a man we loved with all our hearts begin to turn into a monster that we tried to dodge at every opportunity?

As I was growing older, I was soon able to recognize what was happening to our "happy home." My father was destroying our family. At one of my birthday parties, my intoxicated father arrived unexpectedly. In front of all my friends and brothers, he beat me. I was so embarrassed that I did not want to interact with my friends for the rest of the party. My mother and god brother came into the room where I was hiding and assured me that all would be fine. It was at that moment that I started to hate my father. I felt that he didn't like me and that he resented me. Now that I had recognized his pattern of behavior, I began to notice the blatant disrespect for my mother and his mistreatment of my brothers and me.

Soon, the problems of our family started to extend past the walls of our home. My brothers and I were continually embarrassed as my parents began to engage in fistfights and loud arguments in public, outside of our house, and in the hallways of our three- family home. Additionally, my mother began to follow my father when he left the house to see if he was cheating on her. She detested my father and told my brothers and me that we shouldn't be like him.

As children, we were scared every day.

A war zone had developed in the Gordon household. As children, we were scared every day. The unstable situation was too much for our little hearts to handle, but as the famous anonymous quote states, "What doesn't kill you only makes you stronger."

As time progressed, it felt as if a gray cloud was over our lives. There weren't any more Pizza Hut outings, the trips to Grandpa's shop became less frequent, and there weren't as many high-fives from my father at night. These memories were now replaced with yelling, fighting, and beatings. Once in a while, the gray cloud that loomed over our family would allow some sunlight to appear. When these sunny days came, my brothers and I cherished them because we knew that they wouldn't last forever. But on one particular day, the sunlight beamed its rays on my understanding which gave me a *moment of clarity*.

3

MY SON HOLD
DEATH FOR ME

I remember my father was in an unusually good mood on a warm summer day. He was off from work and decided he wanted to do something with his family. However, before we went on this family outing, my father said we had to stop at the famous BBQ restaurant Brothers which was around the corner. Oddly, my father didn't want to walk; he insisted that we drive to Brothers instead.

"Rah, come with me to pick up some things before we head out."

I really didn't want to go because it was so hot and Dad's car had leather seats with no air conditioner. In fact, I am getting hot just reminiscing about the day. I hopped in the car wearing my shorts and t-shirt and immediately jumped out because the leather seat seemingly burned my skin.

"Dad, why don't you keep the windows down? It's hot in there!"

"Boy, get your ass in the car and be a man!" he replied. My father definitely had a way with words.

After driving down the street for a couple of minutes, my dad parked his car and began to exchange hands and conversation with some of his friends. My father returned to the car and gave me a simple smile.

"You good?" It was one of his normal phrases of conversation.

I replied with a nod, and he turned the car's ignition to head to Brothers. As we were travelling to the BBQ restaurant, my father began looking in the rear view mirror. I looked back and noticed a police officer following our car. My father was tense, but he seemed somewhat relieved because we were already in front of Brothers. He waited for about two minutes so that the officer could pass, and then he began to give me instructions.

I looked back and noticed a police officer following our car. My father was tense . . .

"Rah, I want you to hold on to something for me. I don't care who comes to this car, do not let them have it. Okay?"

"Yes," I replied.

"I want you to close your eyes and open your hands. Do not open your eyes until I tell you to," he continued.

I followed his instructions because I knew by the tone in his voice that he was serious. The light might become dim and the gray clouds might come early on this sunny day if I failed to adhere to his directions. When he saw that my eyes were closed completely, he began to pour small solid objects into my hand. He then closed my hand and told me to grip the objects more tightly. Pleased that I had followed his instructions, he instructed me to open my eyes.

"I don't care who comes to this car, don't open your hand. And I don't want you to look in your hand either. Do you hear me boy?" he demanded.

"Yes, Daddy, I won't open my hand for anyone," I responded.

My father then proceeded out of the car and towards Brothers. I watched him disappear into BBQ restaurant, and I waited on my curiosity to take over. I began guessing what could be in my hand. I started playing with the pressure that I had on my grip and concluded that a little peek wouldn't hurt. I quickly opened my hand and viewed colorful tops that held white powder in a very small capsule. Now, I was considered a geek by my fellow classmates, so I started using context clues to determine what was in my hand. Suddenly, it dawned on me. These were the things that were on the poster in school that said, "Say No to Drugs."

I quickly opened my hand and viewed colorful tops that held white powder in a very small capsule.

"*Drugs . . . Daddy . . . Daddy does drugs!*" I remember saying to myself in the hot car.

As soon as I exclaimed my realization, my father ran across the street to get into the car. After he entered, he asked me to close my eyes and open my hand. I felt him take every capsule out of my small and sweaty palm.

"Did you open your hand?" he asked. "No," I replied.

I immediately turned to stare out my door window. I couldn't look my father in the face because I just realized that he used drugs.

4

KIDS ON
THE ROOF

After I realized what was being hidden from me, I came to the conclusion that not only was my father using drugs, but my mother was using them as well. I didn't tell anyone what happened because I felt I would be embarrassed and no one would believe me. Those were two things that I did not want to occur.

As time progressed, the gray cloud I felt and feared became darker. My brothers and I would watch our father beat our mother to the floor while he was looking for money. We would watch and hear them argue repeatedly over things that probably were not major issues. At times, we would fake that we were asleep so we wouldn't be mistreated by my father. It was a crazy situation that no child or young person should have to endure.

I vividly remember a Friday evening when my parents engaged in a huge fight. My mother was thrown into the door by my father who was high. As my mother tried to rise from the floor, my father hit her again. He attempted to get to the front door, but my mother managed to regain her footing and strike him in the face while he walked down the hallway stairs. Filled with rage, he turned around and grabbed her by the neck. He ran her entire body to the door, and after slamming into the hard door, she fell in pain to the floor.

My brothers and I began yelling, crying, and panicking because my mother was hurt. As my father looked at her, he began to yell and called her all types of derogatory names. Suddenly, my mother, who seemed as if she was not going to lose this fight, retrieved a long meat knife. Despite blood running down her face, her determination and strong will remained.

My mother and father squared off in the middle of the kitchen floor. As my mother swung the knife . . .

My mother and father squared off in the middle of the kitchen floor. As my mother swung the knife, my father attacked her, but she cut his neck. He retreated and realized he was bleeding. He assailed her again, but she was quicker and sliced his forearm.

As my father attempted to leave the house, my mother dropped the knife and began chasing him. In the mix of it all, my brothers and I engaged in a long conversation with a friend I will call Silence. But as soon as Silence was finished talking to us, my father returned to the house instead of my mother. I concluded that my mother left the house because she was tired of my father beating her. She left us on that Friday night with a man who was cut on his neck with a butcher knife and had no remorse for hitting a woman he called his wife.

When my father returned to the house, my brothers and I were already in our rooms waiting to see what might happen to us. But our father told us to go to sleep because it was past our bedtime. I don't recall the exact time, but it must have been late in the evening because my youngest brothers went immediately to sleep. After a while, I finally dozed into sleep.

As sort of a brother hierarchy, our sleeping arrangement was that the two eldest brothers were on the top bunk bed while the two youngest were at the bottom. Early in the morning at around 2:38 a.m., I was awakened by a beating from our father. As he beat my brothers and me in our bunk beds, he screamed in rage.

I was hurt mentally, physically, emotionally, and spiritually. I tossed and turned asking, "GOD, why me?"

"Where is your mother?"

"We don't know," we frantically replied in unison.

Despite our genuine reply, he continued to beat us because he was so high that he didn't care if we were telling the truth.

The beatings continued for about an hour as my father relentlessly questioned us about our mother's whereabouts. Finally, the beatings subsided, we were sent back to sleep, and my brothers dozed. But who could go back to sleep with the fear of physical torture at any moment? I couldn't do it! I was hurt mentally, physically, emotionally, and spiritually. I tossed and turned asking, *"GOD, why me?"*

This was it for me. I couldn't live in this situation any-more, so I jumped down from my bunk bed and walked to the window. My brothers were still sleeping when I began to open the window and screen. As I began to climb out the window, my brother, Janvier, awoke.

"Rah, what are you doing?" he asked.

"I am running away to grandma and grandpa's house,"
I replied.

As I said this, Janvier watched me climb on the roof.
I stood there with my arms stretched out looking down
at the ground beneath me. I kept hesitating
because we were on the second floor, and I
was only about nine years old. I was small
in size, so everything looked too high, but
I felt no one was able to help me but my
grandparents.

*R*ight before *I was going to leap, I looked back in the window and saw my little brothers sleeping.*

Time passed slowly as I contemplated
my situation and built the courage to jump.

Right before I was going to leap, I looked
back in the window and saw my little brothers sleeping.
Janvier was still awake and decided to get off the bed. He
ran over to me at the window, and I asked him to push
me off the roof. Instead, Janvier gave me a look that only
those who go through struggles with someone would be
able to offer.

"Rah, don't jump. I don't want to push you."

I told him that the only way to leave this horrible
situation was for me to run to our grandparents' house by
jumping off the roof. But my little brother had a different
view in mind. Immediately, he asked me to come in the
house and told me that we would get through these hard
times together. I felt his words so much that I didn't even
second guess him. We were brothers and when we needed
each other, we were there to support.

I came into the house, and climbed up to my top bunk.
I then leaned over and hit my two little brothers on the

bottom bunk (which made them angry), and I fell asleep.

Author's Note: Years later I went by this house and realized that if I had jumped, I would have never survived the fall. I would have probably died instantly. I am forever grateful to my brother for helping me the way that he did. Even though he was very young and may not have remembered the entire situation, he was a true brother in a moment of pain.

5

WHITNEY

At some point, my parents split, and my mother was left with four young boys. We couldn't live on South 10th Street anymore, so we started living with family members. We moved from house to house each week. Soon, we noticed how we would be in the park for hours and then fall asleep in the car. My mother played it off so well that we didn't realize we were homeless at first. It was when we began living in shelters and taking showers with people who slept nearby Penn Station in Newark, New Jersey, that I arrived at the conclusion that we were homeless.

We slept in almost every shelter in Newark. Those were some hard times. I remember rushing so we could eat at the soup kitchen before it closed. Likewise, our clothes were from the Salvation Army. I couldn't tell you what my style was, but I would go to school thinking I was "fly" (sharply dressed). I would have on purple pants, a green shirt, non-matching socks, and some knock off name brand boots. I had a Kanye West mentality for a homeless kid! *"Can't tell me nothing!"*

I remember one of the shelters that we stayed in when I was in the 5th grade. The shelter was located in downtown Newark, and it was called The Apostle House. During the holidays, the staff would arrange special events and dinners.

To my great joy, we were surprised by Bobby Brown and
Whitney Houston.

I don't remember the exact day, but it was around 4:00
p.m. at the shelter, and we were scheduled to go to the
Terrace Ballroom in downtown Newark to the
holiday event hosted by Whitney Houston
and Bobby Brown. All of the shelter families
boarded buses which transported us to the
event location.

*I*t was like a
dream to see a
huge Christmas
tree with
hundreds of gifts
surrounding it.

Once we arrived at the ballroom, there
were other families present from various
shelters in the city. Christmas gifts for us
were all over the ballroom. It was like a dream to see a
huge Christmas tree with hundreds of gifts surrounding it.
When it was time for dinner, we were seated at a table that
provided food we wished we could eat every day. Soon,
announcements were made that Bobby and Whitney
would be arriving within the next hour. One could feel the
excitement in the ballroom, and everyone started talking
with great anticipation about meeting the two worldwide
celebrities.

Although my brothers and I lived in the shelter with
our mother, I could only think about my father while we
were at the event. He was an avid Bobby Brown fan. He
always had us get Gumby style haircuts like Bobby Brown,
and we always heard his music in my father's car. I thought
it would be clever to stand outside the ballroom so that I
would be able to get their autographs when they arrived.

After a while, a limousine arrived with the celebrity
couple. I ran back inside the ballroom and yelled with

excitement that they were coming. The families began to get noisy, and the anticipation in the ballroom increased.

When the couple arrived in the ballroom, they mingled with folks and took many pictures with several families. But as the event was concluding, I still didn't have Bobby Brown's autograph for my father, so I ran over to their table and asked Bobby for an autograph. I told him how my father loved him and how I was going to be a star.

The families began to get noisy, and the anticipation in the ballroom increased.

As I was telling him this, the couple's managers said it was time for them to leave, but Whitney insisted on staying until I got my autograph. I ran around looking for a pen and a piece of paper. When I came back, they signed the paper and smiled at me.

"You have such a beautiful smile," Whitney said.

After signing the autograph for me, Bobby and Whitney left the Terrace Ballroom to much applause. Personally, I was on cloud nine. Despite my young age, I recognized the enormity of what had just occurred. I had a conversation with two individuals who changed music, style, and had an influence on people's lives. It was an amazing honor that I will never forget!

6

PROJECT BABIES

Our final shelter was at the YMCA in downtown Newark. After our stay there, we moved to Prince Street Projects. Younger generations may not remember these projects in Newark, but if you have ever watched *New Jack City* or *New Jersey Drive,* you can imagine the environment. We lived in those projects for quite some time. Our family then moved to 88 Barkley Terrace, which were the smaller projects behind Prince Street Projects.

At Barkley Terrace, we lived in a one bedroom apartment without any furniture. There was a bed, but that was where my mother and her boyfriend slept. As a result, my brothers and I slept on black trash bags that held the clothes we received from the shelters. It was common for us to share the washcloths, towels, and clothes so it never bothered us.

There were also times when we washed our clothes in the sink and dried them in the oven. We used a wire hanger to hold our damp socks, and we placed them in front of the oven with the door down to dry the socks. On other occasions, we placed our underwear and socks on the radiator because its heat was always better than the oven heat. However, this faster drying method was not without consequences; the radiator often left rusty lines on our undergarments.

Sometimes, my mother would not be able to arrive home from work prior to my brothers and me getting home from school. She would give me the welfare card to get food to eat. Instead, my brothers and I used the card to pick the apartment lock so we wouldn't have to wait for her to come home. My brothers and I always planned and strategized our daily survival. It was our street smarts on Prince and Barkley Streets that instilled us with the power to endure our family's struggles.

. . . my brothers and I used the card to pick the apartment lock so we wouldn't have to wait for her to come home.

During the time my family was living in the projects, I was in the 6th grade at Louis A. Spencer Elementary School. I was a smart student, and I was selected for the gifted and talented program. Specifically, the program was designed for students who demonstrated accelerated learning relative to the total student body. I was given a letter for my mother to sign so I could participate in the program. However, because of my mother's situation, she was unable to attend the required parent-teacher orientation meeting. I was hurt as I had worked hard to be selected for this program. As a result, my mother and I got in a major argument, and I told her how I didn't think she cared for me. I was so devastated that I could not feel happy with my life at such a young age.

My mother was hurt when I told her my feelings. She also told me that my father didn't care for us and he didn't want to be involved in any part of our lives.

"You're lying," I said. "I don't want to live with you anymore. I want to live with dad."

My mother directed me to the phone to call and tell my father that I wanted to live with him. As I stormed downstairs to the payphone, I remembered the famous commercial to dial collect, "1-800-C-O-L-L-E-C-T." I began to feel happy because I was sure my father would tell me to pack my things and that he was on his way to get me.

I made the call, and I patiently waited for the operator to ask my father if he would accept my call. To my surprise, his reply was, "NO." He would not accept my call!

> *I needed money, food, and a way to control the situation around me . . .*

"I HATE YOU," I yelled with frustration.

I waited another hour and called him again. This time, he accepted my call. I told him the situation with my mother and how I needed his support and love.

"Dad, can I live with you?"

"Not right now. I have my girlfriend and her kids," he replied.

That day was so painful for me. I felt lost, but I knew I had the brilliance of a genius while living in the gutter.

The incident was a life-changing event for me; I felt now that it was I against the world. I needed money, food, and a way to control the situation around me, so I started bagging groceries. Following school, I would immediately go to the supermarket to begin work. It became a daily routine just so I could eat because I knew I couldn't depend on my mother to provide such basic necessities for me.

However, I started to have competition from the other project kids who desired to work as grocery baggers as well.

I had to be smart. I had to be creative. I started thinking of ways to beat my competition.

I began running from school instead of walking with friends. I would often arrive at the supermarket a half hour earlier than the store opening time. Also, after careful analysis, I would take the express lanes rather than the general lanes. I recognized that on the first of the month, customers would have two carts full of food which ultimately reduced my flow rate of customers. If I bagged groceries in the express lane instead, there was easier work with a higher number of customers. Additionally, shoppers with fewer items generally meant they had more change available to give.

During our time in the projects, my brothers and I began to see things differently.

My strategy worked so well that I was able to buy groceries for my family. At times, I would make $30.00, and it would be sufficient to buy food to feed my brothers, mother, and her boyfriend. I felt proud to provide for my family. Besides my mother, no one else was doing it.

During our time in the projects, my brothers and I began to see things differently. While I was bagging groceries, my two youngest brothers ran drug bags for the local drug dealer.

My brother Janvier was neutral to the different directions of my two youngest brothers and me, but he was often quiet and observant to what was happening. When I would come home, Janvier would give me updates on my younger brothers, and when we were all together, we would discuss these events. Most people wouldn't understand the mechanic of our world, but that is why my brothers and I were mostly alone.

7

VIBRATIONS
OF AN ANGEL

As time progressed, my brothers and I developed health issues that were due to stress and abuse. While these experiences were painful alone, such health complications only made our situation more difficult. For example, Alfonso was placed on various medications because of his diagnosis. However, despite his health issues, he was a very brilliant and dynamic child.

An aunt that the entire family was close to passed away from cancer. The entire family was saddened, and we all expressed our grief differently in the situation. After the funeral, we gathered at our grandparents' home, and I sat on the porch just thinking.

Suddenly, I heard people yelling in the backyard. I ran back to the rear of the house to see the cause of the outburst, and I saw Alfonso venting with aggression, pain, and hurt. My family tried to calm him, but he just seemed to get louder. Alfonso stated he was leaving and would not return. He started towards the fence, and when he got closer to the gate, he ran in escape.

Immediately, everyone began yelling and some started to cry. I was near my grandmother at the time.

"Go get your brother," she said with a direct stare and a calm voice.

Without hesitation, I ran after Alfonso. We ran at top speed in the middle of the street before I was able to catch up with him. I grabbed and hugged him so that he couldn't escape. Suddenly, he collapsed in my arms, and his eyes began to roll to the back of his head as tears ran down his cheek. I fell to the ground with him in my arms.

> *Suddenly, he collapsed in my arms, and his eyes began to roll to the back of his head as tears ran down his cheek.*

"No, Fonso, don't do this to me!"

I began yelling for help in the middle of the street while crying harder than I ever had before.

"Alfonso don't die. Come on!"

My mother saw us from a distance and started running. As she approached, I tried to hold Alfonso's tongue so he wouldn't swallow it, but when my mother arrived, she started pulling him to her.

"Stop Mommy, you are killing him. Stop please!" I yelled some more, but she held him as he was experiencing a seizure.

I broke down on the curb watching my mother hold her young son in the street. When the ambulance arrived, I walked back to my grandparents' house. My grandmother came out the back of the house, and I fell into her arms with tears flowing like a river down my face.

"I can't take it anymore Grandma."

"Rah, you gotta be strong. You are the oldest. Do you hear me?" she said as she held me tightly.

She whispered in my ear that I would be fine and that I needed to stand strongly because my brothers needed me. While the pain of the incident almost brought me to my own breaking point, my grandmother's words gave me the foundation to hold me up.

Once my grandmother and I finished talking, I went inside to be by myself. More family arrived and some family left.

However, the memory of the day with Alfonso vibrated my world.

8

COME WALK
WITH ME

At some point, my mother couldn't handle rearing all four boys, so my father decided to become involved again in our lives. I was going into the 7th grade when my brothers and I moved in again with my father. But at this age and time of my life, the love I once had for my father was almost gone. The dark clouds and rain we experienced with him earlier in our lives were times that my brothers and I tried to remove from our memories. It was a place that I did not want to return.

At the same time, I never knew until my college years that there was an ulterior motive for my father's new willingness to support us. Figuratively speaking, my brothers and I were walking around with dollar signs over our heads. A single parent with four kids can receive benefits from the government. Nevertheless, despite this additional income, my brothers and I never received the necessary supplies for school unless we received assistance from family members.

When we moved in with our father, we resided at 58 Nairn Place, which was off Clinton Avenue in Newark. Our home had thirteen people living there to include me, my three brothers, my father, his girlfriend, her son, her three daughters, and her three grandchildren. Unfortunately, there was only one bathroom in the house. When everyone had to use the bathroom after dinner, a line actually formed in the hallway.

I transferred to Hawthorne Avenue School, and I began to research possible high school locations. I made many friends at school and within the community, and these friendships gave my life joy and excitement. We would have house parties and played various hood games that made time pass by quickly throughout the day.

She asked if I attended church regularly, and I replied that I did not.

One memory from this time in my life touches my heart. Deshae and Earl, two of my closest new friends at that time, went to church every Sunday. One Sunday, I met their legal guardian, Ms. Lyons, who was in her late fifties. She asked if I attended church regularly, and I replied that I did not. She told me that she would like to see me in church because it was "the place to be." I agreed that I would go the following Sunday with Deshae and Earl.

After that first Sunday, I attended Hopewell Baptist Church in Newark every week. I walked from my house to church each Sunday at 6:30 a.m. just so I could arrive in time for Bible School which started at 8:00 a.m. I only owned one suit and a pair of hand-me- down shoes, so I wore the same outfit to church every Sunday. When the suit needed to be cleaned, I washed it in the bathtub and hung it up to dry in my bedroom window. It was my only Sunday suit, and I was proud to wear it.

The walk to church was long during the winter and even longer during the summer. I wore my suit through winter storms and during summer heat waves. When I wore the suit, I was headed to church.

Since the walk took about an hour and a half to church in often less than desirable conditions, I sometimes questioned my reason for attending.

When the winter months brought heavy snow storms, I wore my favorite lumber coat that didn't have any buttons to keep me warm on the walk to church. Ms. Lyons, a church friend, and a church deacon questioned me about a coat, and I told them I didn't own one.

Early one Sunday evening, my friend Earl came over to my house to ask if I could come by Ms. Lyons's house. My father approved, and I ran down the block with Earl to her house. When we arrived, Ms. Lyons was waiting for me in the kitchen with the deacon from church. He was holding a bag which read "Perry Ellis."

Ms. Lyons and the deacon smiled at me as they handed me the bag. After reaching inside, I removed a brand new winter coat with a price tag that read $110.00. I smiled broadly while trying to remain humble and grateful. I hugged both of them. They commented to me that they were intrigued with my faithfulness to God at such a young age and noted how I attended church even if my friends did not. They prayed for me, and after thanking them again, I returned home with my new coat. I continued to walk to church in the winter cold, but now I did so with a new coat and a new way of being happy.

9

THE BASEMENT
IN HOODAVILLE

My father was having difficulty maintaining our house at Nairn Place, and he felt that we needed a change of space. Additionally, we were too crowded with so many people living under the same roof in the smaller house.

As a result, we moved to Martins Avenue which was adjacent to Tremont Avenue in Newark during the middle of my 8th grade year. Specifically, the area was known as Hoodaville. We moved to a house that was directly across the street from the graveyard. It also had a great side view of Bradley Court Projects, better known as "Tombstone."

I transferred to Camden Middle School, and I soon made friends with people who are still some of my greatest friends to this day. I was still interested in sports, and I played on the basketball team with and against some of the nation's top basketball players of my generation. However, during the final months of my 8th grade year, my art teacher, Ms.

East, involved me with the Art Club. As I became interested in art, my involvement helped me meet the required standards to pass the high school exam in art. I was accepted as an art major.

In the beginning, I really enjoyed my high school experience. At the same time, I dreaded returning home after the end of each school day. I would find every possible way to stay away from home until it was time to have dinner and be by myself.

I was motivated by the sounds of hip hop, and I was becoming more connected with the lyrics of the songs.

When I was at home, I stayed secluded in my room just listening to music. I was a big fan of Biggie Smalls and Tupac. I printed the lyrics to their songs and posted them on my wall next to their poster pictures. I remember having Raekwon's purple tape bumping heavy in my speakers while waiting for the debut of Wu-Tang Clan's new video "Wu- Tang Forever" on MTV. The video felt like a movie to me when I first saw it on television. I was motivated by the sounds of hip hop, and I was becoming more connected with the lyrics of the songs.

One day, I was listening to my music when my father's girlfriend announced that Alfonso had been suspended from school. My brothers and I knew that our father was going to beat Alfonso once he returned home. We were scared for Alfonso, but it wasn't something for which we could prepare.

When my father arrived home and was told of Alfonso's suspension, he immediately went to Alfonso's bedroom and beat him profusely. My father stripped down Alfonso to his underwear and viciously hit his chest, back, and legs. It was extremely difficult to watch my brother endure this pain. We felt helpless. We were scared to help our brother because our father was our master. It was as if we were his slaves, and beating of slaves was common on the Gordon Plantation.

After my father beat Alfonso until he literally couldn't walk, he dragged him down the basement staircase. He instructed Alfonso to stay and sleep in the basement until he was told otherwise. Two dogs accompanied Alfonso in the basement, which had no heat and no bathroom. There was a bed, but that is where the dogs slept. There were a few old blankets too, but who knows where those came from.

We sometimes sneaked him food to eat if my father felt he wasn't worthy of eating.

Alfonso stayed in the basement close to a month and a half. His routine was to come upstairs, get dressed, go to school, come home, and go back to the basement. We sometimes sneaked him food to eat if my father felt he wasn't worthy of eating. Likewise, we often whispered to him through the chained basement door.

I sometimes blamed myself for this incident because I felt I could have done more to protect my brother. I would not wish a situation like this on my worst enemies. My heart hurt as a big brother and as a human being. At the same time, I was affected mentally, and the incident caused me to become increasingly rebellious.

10

LET ME
SHOW YOU LOVE

During the time in which Alfonso stayed in the basement, my brother Isaiah got into trouble as well. When my father learned about Isaiah's behavior, he decided to implement the same punishment for Isaiah as he did for Alfonso. Now, only Janvier and I remained in the house while our baby brothers were in the basement.

But it wasn't long before Janvier and I joined our younger brothers in the basement as well. When I was sent to the basement, I could not understand how my younger brothers were able sleep there. I slept on top of the washing machine with my favorite lumber jacket. When we needed heat to fight the dampness and cold of the basement, we turned on the dryer for a few minutes and placed our head and hands inside.

My brothers slept on the floor or even slept in the car because we were able to get into the garage. During the long hours in the basement, my brothers and I would talk about our future and how we wanted to live. We all said, *"I can't wait to get big!"*

Conversations like these helped maintain our spirits. We were each other's keepers. We fought, laughed, played, and loved each other as brothers, but sometimes because of our dark circumstances, we couldn't enjoy our brotherly bonding the way other brothers probably did.

I was becoming tired and fed up with the continual abuse that my brothers and I received. I was a freshman in high school dealing with normal teen issues, and combined with the child abuse at home, I was hurting. However, through all of this negativity, I was still able to smile in public. I didn't want anybody involved or aware of my problems, and if I had an issue, then I was going to have to solve it. However, my father always had a way of trying to change this mindset.

I didn't want anybody involved or aware of my problems, and if I had an issue, then I was going to have to solve it.

My father called me in his room one day and told me that I needed to stay home from school to pay the electricity bill with documentation from the welfare office. I was resistant to his demand because I had not missed a day in school, and now he wanted me to just so I could do his job. I explained to him that I had a test, but he told me that paying the electric bill was more important than a high school art literature test.

As a result, I did not attend school, and I missed my test. I became angry when I could not pay the bill because I was a minor. I told my father what happened when he came home, but he insisted I stay home again the following day. He said he would make a call from work in order for me to pay the bill.

I stayed home from school for a second day, and I still couldn't pay the bill because of my age. I became very worried; my father had given me a task which I was not able to complete. He felt that I was the man of the house when he was gone and what he couldn't do I should handle. He always instructed me to be strong in my position and to never allow other people get over on me. Although he was abusive, he managed to instill me with life lessons that I still live by to this day.

At that moment, however, I was more focused on his possible actions when he returned home. Instead of watching television in the living room, I went to my room to listen and watch for his arrival. When he did return, he checked to see if my two brothers were in the basement, and then he went to his bedroom to talk to his girlfriend. After a few minutes, it became quiet in the house, and I began to think he wouldn't call for me. But I was wrong.

Although he was abusive, he managed to instill me with life lessons that I still live by to this day.

"Rahfeal, get your ass in here!"

I raised enough guts, poked out my chest, and walked to his room calmly. I knew what happened next would be contentious.

His rampage commenced. "Rah did you pay the light bill?"

"No Dad. I couldn't pay for it because of my age. They said it didn't matter if you called," I replied.

He gave a stare as though he was so disgusted with me and he was hurting just by looking at me.

"Why do you act like a bitch?" he yelled. "I tell you to do one thing and you can't even do that."

I looked at him and knew that I was finished with this man whom I called father. He told me to get out of his room, and my emotion began to spill over.

"I can't take this shit no more!" I yelled. I began to walk out of his room. "What did you say?"

All I could do was go right back at him with words. "Leave me the fuck alone!"

Without hesitation, my father immediately ran my head into the side of the door and then into the hallway wall. I tried to run to my room, but I had stupidly locked myself out my own room. Suddenly, my father helped me open the door by ramming my body against it.

*E*veryone *began crowding around telling me to stop, but my brothers were cheering me on.*

Everything was happening so fast. After I was rammed into the door, I don't remember anything but seeing black. I started yelling and threw back my right fist which ended up across my father's face. My father hit the floor, and I instinctively jumped on top of him. I grabbed him around his neck and began suffocating him. Everyone began crowding around telling me to stop, but my brothers were cheering me on. My father tried to flip me over to get control, but by the time he tried, I was already loose from the tussle and started running for the door.

As I ran, all I could think about was getting to my grandparents' house. I ran as fast as I could, but before I could get to the corner, I was out of breath. I sat in the street and watched as Janvier came running to me.

"Hey Rah! Yo, you knocked daddy out, but he wants to see you," he said.

My mind was running all over the place. I composed myself and headed back to our house with Janvier. When I got upstairs, everyone was there while my father was standing in the middle of the floor. He told me he loved me and that he didn't mean to hurt me.

After he apologized, he directed me to my room which I was more than happy to hear rather than his words of forgiveness. I turned on my CD player and began playing Biggie Smalls "Juicy." I felt good, and I believed that our family situation would now be different.

Later on, my father knocked on my bedroom door. I remember that "Picture Me Rolling" by Tupac Shakur was playing when I heard his taps on the door. He apologized again and gave me a hug. After a few minutes, his girl-friend's daughter walked past my room.

"You know this is my oldest boy? He acts up, but I love him very much." She smiled with a puzzled look.

"The only reason you are saying this is because he knocked you!" she said.

I smiled and then went back to my room and blasted the *Ready to Die* album by Biggie
Smalls.

"No one has never been as
broke as me, and I like that."

—B.I.G.

11

WHAT IS
THAT WEIRD SMELL

As time progressed, my brothers and I enjoyed our freedom outside of the basement. We listened to music on the porch during spring and summer days while watching the beautiful view of the cemetery that scared us during Halloween.

At times, our father hung out with us on the porch and cracked jokes. He had his moments of being fun and full of life. We were able to see God in him when heaven seemed to be within our home. It was those moments that we prayed for so we wouldn't see the clouds forming that dimmed the heavenly light around us.

One day, my father pulled up to the porch and asked me to join him in his car. He was smoking his favorite Newport cigarettes. He quickly asked if everything was good, and I nodded in affirmation. He stated that he needed me to do a favor for him, and I asked what it was that he needed. By this time, I was a little man because after the fight, he showed me more respect and gave me space to grow. He started with hesitation in his voice, and then he asked me to buy drugs for him from my friends that hustled around the corner. I was so shocked that I was at a loss for words.

I thought for a moment before I responded, and I began to see him as a man fading away.

"No," I said with a tremble in my voice.

My father asked again, and I repeated my response a second time but with more confidence in my voice. I started thinking how embarrassed I would be if I bought drugs from my friends. What would they say about me? What respect would I have for myself if I did do it? I immediately jumped out of the car and went back on the porch, and my father drove somewhere else to purchase his street medication.

I started thinking how embarrassed I would be if I bought drugs from my friends.

A few hours passed, and my father returned to the house. It was late by this time, but it was the beginning of the weekend, so it was permissible to still be outside. My father went inside the house, and then returned to the porch to go to his hangout spot. He asked me to come with him, so I joined him in the car. When we arrived at his hangout spot that I had known for quite some time, I decided to stay outside. After a while, I went into the house and was greeted by faces I had never seen before.

As I sat on the sofa, I smelled this indescribable odor that made my nose twitch. Once the smell became the aroma of the house, people were walking around like zombies and talking wildly. I sat on the couch and acted as though I was watching television, but I knew what they were doing. I remember the quote that was told to me, "A smart man can play dumb, but a dumb man can't play smart."

My father came from out of the kitchen and asked if I was all right. I said I was, and then he went outside. He returned a few hours later and went back to the kitchen. Once he did his medication that consumed the air with a weird death smell, he returned and looked at me. He told me he was going home, but he would be back soon.

. . . he was actually leaving me in a crack house to rear myself.

When he left, I had a hunch that he did not plan on returning. In fact, he was actually leaving me in a crack house to rear myself. He must have felt that I was able to take care of myself, or maybe he thought I could focus on becoming a better man than he. Nevertheless, he made a point that he was through with taking care of me as his son. I was 15 years old when he left me at the place I eventually called home.

12

CANDY KINGPIN

After a while, I began moving from home to home. Deserted by my father, I had to develop strategies for my daily survival and to generate income. As a result, I commenced my journey as an entrepreneur and leader.

I didn't know too much about business plans and all the legal documentation that came with establishing a real business. I still felt that I could be a businessman while in high school. I established a company called Infinite Productions. My first business project to create revenue involved hosting a bake sale after school. My first investor for this business project was my grandmother. She packed me and my team into her Cadillac and drove us to the bakery to buy cakes and cookies. The project was a huge success and we raised close to $112. We were rolling in money!

The business I started became a staple at my high school during my time there. It was through Infinite Productions that we were able to host trips when the school board said they didn't have money to help us experience the things we wanted. We hosted bus trips to the New Jersey beaches on weekends, went to the Great Adventures Amusement Park, and held barbeques. It was great.

As with all businesses, there were shortcomings and moments when things didn't go so well. When things were tough monetarily, I met with my mother, (just a reminder that I wasn't living with her), and she would take me with a large group of kids to ask for money at the entrances of various highways in Newark. My mother would have us do this for some old church. We would have to go back to the church if we wanted to receive our individual funds. We kept half of whatever was donated in our cups; the other half went to the church we were raising money for. In the beginning, I was embarrassed, but I really needed the money. I wasn't working, and as a teenager, you get tired of people picking on you due to how you dress or because you have no money to participate in various cool activities.

. . . as a teenager, you get tired of people picking on you due to how you dress . . .

After school, I would hurry to the bus and go meet my mother so we could head out. On one of those days, my best friend at the time was telling me how he also needed money. It was the first time I shared with him what I was doing after school besides trying to organize bus rides and bake sales. He tagged along with me to see if he could do it. After about 10 minutes, he sat on the side of the road and refused to go out to ask for money. I was incredibly embarrassed because he was my best friend and he wouldn't do it. Of course, a few more friends found out. I had to live with the fact that I was truly begging for money.

The last straw was when I decided to quit playing basketball because I was only getting my playtime with the junior varsity team. I had much more free time after quitting the team. So, I went back on the corner with that group and did what I knew would help put money in my pocket. Maybe a few weeks later, my coach pulled up to the light before getting on the highway and I knocked on his window to ask for a donation. Boy, were we both surprised. His expression held both confusion and sympathy. Mine conveyed a sense of exposure and discomfort. He held up traffic to ask me a few questions, then said something along the lines of, he better see me back in the gym during the next season.

I knew numerous drug dealers, too, as I was growing up, because they were the celebrities . . .

After that, I quit wearing wrinkled shirts with faded writing on them just to get a few dollars from begging for a church I never attended.

I had a large number of friends, and I was adept at keeping my personal life private. At the same time, I still had to confront the outside world after the school bell rang. I had a few close friends who were in a similar situation to mine, but they believed selling drugs was the remedy to their problems.

I knew numerous drug dealers, too, as I was growing up, because they were the celebrities in the 'hood. They drove the fastest cars, had the hottest women, and wore the coolest chains. They gave us money to eat when our parents didn't, and they were the cheerleaders at our summer basketball games. To poor young boys, they were easy and available role models.

As a result, many of my old friends started hustling for big-time drug dealers, but I couldn't be involved with that business and lifestyle. I didn't understand the mechanics of the success rate. I only saw two results: death or jail. Neither of those options was any motivation for me. Consequently, I began to lose friendships with those whom I had considered close. I guess when a person needs money, friendship becomes a casualty in the drug game.

While their industry was illegal, there were many business lessons that could be learned . . .

Although I didn't work for the drug dealers, I still studied and conversed with them. I was interested in them because, in a way, they were entrepreneurs. While their industry was illegal, there were many business lessons that could be learned from these drug dealers from the hardcore inner-city.

One of my street mentors took a liking to me due to my character and business mindset at a very young age. He would pick me up from school and share life lessons that are still relevant to my life today. I never hesitated to ask questions or felt scared to question what I saw while spending time with him.

I admired him for the respect he commanded and received. He was direct and always told me to handle my business. He never wanted me to take anything personally because when it comes to making money and being a boss, people are emotional; not the business. The goal is to make money by supplying the demand. Period.

One night, he asked if I would like to ride with him to meet with one of his business partners. I was cool with it and didn't feel the need to be alarmed in any type of way. I was sure about one thing, he wasn't ever going to put me in harm's way. That's just something I felt in my gut. He was one of the big brothers I never had.

I felt the urge to ask, "Can I ask you a question?"

He responded, "Sure Rah, ask whatever you have on your mind."

I took a brief moment to reassure myself that it wasn't a stupid question. And then I asked, "Do you have a million dollars or have you counted a million dollars before?" It was one of those moments that I didn't know what would happen or what I'd hear next from my mentor.

He slowly grinned as he stared beyond where we were, as if I asked him a deep question. He then turned to me briefly (because he was driving) and responded, "I don't have a million dollars Rah, but I've definitely gotten close to it."

I nodded with an okay gesture. "I'm going to make you a million dollars one day. I promise you that. I'm going to make you a million dollars."

Once I jotted down all the negativity that I witnessed in my city, I began to substitute it with positive ideas.

My mentor laughed but stopped in all seriousness and said, "You know, I have no doubt you will make that million dollars."

It was moments like this that caused me to stick around my mentors. They believed in me in ways others did not. They were bosses and I wanted to be them. They thought with a business mindset and had an entrepreneurial spirit. That wasn't a common thing among my peers at school.

Many past memories come to mind after sharing this. Another one in particular pushed me to take the leap to make a lot of money while in high school to keep me off the streets. One day, the "king" whom my friends considered their boss approached me. The dealer had considerable influence in my area when I was growing up, and he had most of the young boys in the neighborhood hustling.

"All of your boys hustle for me. When you gonna get down?" "I'm good," I replied.

He smiled as though he was happy with my answer. "You always been different than the rest of your boys. I ain't mad at that though, nah meen?"

I thanked him for the comment, and then the lesson started.

"You seem smart, little homie. You remind me of myself when I was young. I be watching you going to work, playing ball, and with your little brothers. You the oldest, right?"

"Yep," I answered.

"I want to give you something to help as you continue to do your thing," the king said.

I had nothing but time, so I relaxed and let him speak.

"I want you to take everything you think is negative and make it positive. I know what I'm doing isn't a real job in your eyes or to others around you. It's cool, though, because I don't think anyone would be doing this if they didn't have to. But you see how it is out here. So, we gotta do what we gotta do. Check this, I know you've been watching what's been going on out here. Take what you see and make it work for you. If you don't like something, take it out of your studies and put something else in its place so it is substituted with a positive piece."

I understood everything the king was telling me. I had so many ideas that I started writing things down right then. He told me to make my city proud and always recognize the real from the fake. He also said to always deal with people who make things happen. After our talk, I went home and started strategizing my plan to be the kingpin of my city.

Once I jotted down all the negativity I witnessed in my city, I began to substitute it with positive ideas. He'd told me to be the boss and
make money. That was worth considering: *No individual is powerful, great, or respected if there is no confidence or promise in his word.*
it's difficult to help people without money.
I pondered on what I could do to generate
income, and then it hit me.

Instead of being a drug kingpin, I could be the *candy* kingpin. I could make candy my substitute for drugs. Candy wouldn't harm anyone (except for their teeth), everyone wanted it, and nobody was selling it in school. After I had the idea, I jumped quickly on the opportunity.

First, I found a wholesale store that sold candy such as Skittles, Snickers, Kit-Kat, and Twix in bulk. Since I was buying the candy in large quantities, I was able to purchase it at a lower price to later make a profit.

Next, I began to substitute the other pieces of my business for what the king had described. My "city" would be my high school. My streets would be each floor in the school. The mayor would be the principal. The teachers would be the city council members. The police would be the security guards. Wherever I stayed, I would consider the location my honeycomb (that is, my place to prepare products).

Third, I developed and established my strategic distribution plan. I would have other students selling my product (candy). Each grade level, freshmen through seniors, would have two sellers. Likewise, each floor would have a runner in case one of my sellers ran out of candy and needed to be resupplied. This was often the case during lunchtime because there was always a line to purchase snacks.

Now, I had to be smart at times, because students were not allowed to bring candy to school, especially to sell for personal gain. As a result, I "paid off" all the "city council members" and "police" by asking all my teachers and the security guards the type of candy and snacks they enjoyed. I created a list and made sure they had their respective candy fix whenever I was selling in my "city." By doing this, I was able to avoid getting my bags searched when I arrived at school, and therefore, I was able to sell my products in all my classes.

I was as fair as the drug kingpin because I ensured that everyone on the team could eat (make money)—I even had a payroll. Each person who sold candy received 25 cents for each piece sold. In contrast, if he or she damaged my products, lost them, or got them taken by "city officials," the careless seller would have to pay me for the candy. If a seller didn't have the money to do so, he or she would have to work it off by selling my candy until the debt was paid.

My business operated better than I expected. I made as much as $200 to $350 per day, which included money from my after-school job. Out on my own, I was able to make enough money to feed myself, purchase clothing, and go to certain high school functions. I was even able to buy my prom outfit.

I became a kingpin in the city of candy by combining book and street smarts. I achieved the same results as the drug kingpin who told me to make a change. Whenever I reminisce, it amazes me that I chose to sell candy instead of drugs. I was always around drugs, yet still I turned away. You might think I would get looked down upon for my choice. In reality, the man everyone else looked up to respected me for what I was doing!

I kept my word to my street mentor, just like he'd advised me. No individual is powerful, great, or respected if there is no confidence or promise in his word. As I promised the king, I took what was negative in my city and made it positive for me in my own city.

As time went on during the school year, I mastered my business strategies and started to find new opportunities to expand my high school empire. Even if I didn't recognize that I had more confidence, focus, and swag about myself, those around me surely took notice. One of my church mothers who we all called, Sister Barbra, has always been a genuine and beautiful soul from the first time I met her. She took notice of how I was juggling playing on the basketball team and being a young entrepreneur.

One day, I believe it was during a church youth program, Sister Barbra had gotten all the youth who attended the program gifts she believed fit everyone's personality. When it was my turn to receive a gift, she grabbed my hand with a glowing smile and said, "Rah, you are my young business man." She presented me with an NBA basketball briefcase. I was beaming with joy and smiles the whole time. I didn't want a book bag anymore; I had an official briefcase like a real businessman. It was a gift that I have kept with me and still use today!

I would dress up in business attire 1–2 times a week just to match the style of the briefcase. I wore a bookbag and carried my briefcase. I was proud to have it. No student in my entire school showed up with a briefcase. Some of the students at my school laughed at me while others just stared at me as I opened it revealing stacks of money, note-books, business plans, and my homework. Yeah, I was a real boss out there in those high school streets—haha!

One day while getting dressed in the locker room after basketball practice, I got into a debate with one of our star basketball players. We were arguing about who was the better player and who would win if we played one-on-one. Of course, all our teammates added fuel to the fire by pick-ing sides and saying we could find out that night.

We both took the bait and we all had to walk home the same way. It was inevitable that this debate would get set-tled before we all departed. We all lived within short blocks from each other, so we walked together to an empty basket-ball court that was amongst housing projects called, Little Bricks. We had to clear some of the broken glass from the court and keep our eyes open because it was definitely not a place you want to be late night at all.

We decided to play for $20.00 and whoever scored 12 points first, won the game. Now, here is where the lesson happened for me. I had to be a man of my word because my integrity, brand, and reputation were on the line. I lost and had to pay up. I walked to my briefcase, pulled out my checkbook, and proceeded to say, "Can I write you a check?"

Now, let me say I thought I was going to be looked at like a boss. I was prepared to get a look of respect because I had a real bank account and I had a checkbook with my name on it. However, that was definitely not going to be my reality. My teammate looked at me in complete disgust and said, "A check?? Nah bro, I want cash. Who the fuck bets with a check?" At that exact moment everyone burst out laughing hysterically at me. They roasted me for the rest of the night. Only one of my teammates, who was a senior said, "I respect that, but this shit is funny!"

It was one of those moments I realized that no matter what I said, it would only dig a deeper hole for me. There I was, in the middle of the most infamous housing projects in my city and I had the audacity to be betting with bank checks. My teammate was really heated that I didn't have the cash on me. After a while, we all had to depart because it was getting too late and we would have more than just $20.00 to worry about. I ended up agreeing to give him the money the next day once I had my candy workers in motion.

I reflect quite frequently about moments that taught business lessons and how I developed a strategist mindset. Being observant, calculating, moving differently than those around me, and understanding that what is valuable and respected in one world may not be in another.

Ultimately, we all have experiences that become golden, lifelong lessons for us. No matter if we gained them under someone's wings or by hurting our own wings trying to fly, if we look at everything as tool, whether it's in the form of someone teaching us business strategy in the hood, gifting us a briefcase, or giving us the confidence to pull out a checkbook in the middle of the housing projects to cover a bet, I can bet you a million dollars it will all turn out for the greater good of your life. Keep reading and you will see what I mean.

13

YOU'RE NOT
SUPPOSED TO MAKE IT

During my final years of high school, my brothers and I lived together again in my uncle's home. Times were good for us; we had a roof over our heads, we went to church together, and we always had food to eat. My grandmother was still actively involved in our lives during our stay with our Uncle. She also made it clear that she could not over step any boundaries with my uncle because he was our legal guardian.

I was working at Johnny Rockets in the Short Hills Mall while still selling candy at school. Janvier attended Irvington High School and was a "ladies' man." He also enjoyed basketball, which he played almost every day. Alfonso and Isaiah were still in elementary school and attended a gymnastics program called "Flip City" at the Boys & Girls Club. The program kept them off the street, and it was something at which they excelled.

When my grandmother, Janvier, and I would pick up my younger brothers, their coaches would often praise them for their amazing talent. The coaches often spoke about the possibility of them competing in the Junior Olympics and flying to Europe with the Flip City team. We were all excited and thought it was their big break out of the 'hood. I was impressed, and I thought frequently about the great opportunity my younger brothers could have in another country.

However, the strict rules we abided by while living with my uncle precluded this opportunity for my younger brothers. As Alfonso and Isaiah progressed in the Boys & Girls Club, they spent less time at church. But our uncle would not allow any worldly activity to be prioritized over church. "If you live in my house, you will have to go to church," he repeatedly told us.

"If you live in my house, you will have to go to church," he repeatedly told us.

While we understood this important principle, we were in church all the time. We were there all day on Sundays, as we participated in choir rehearsals and other youth activities. We appreciated my uncle's strong advocacy for church, but he was also strict about my younger brothers competing after school and completing their homework; his priorities left little time for theirs. Frankly speaking, my younger brothers were not as interested in church as my uncle would have liked them to be. They had a talent that could take them all over the world, and it was being restricted. The situation was a point of contention, and I struggled with the issue.

Ultimately, my grandmother had to removed my brothers from the Boys & Girls Club because she did not want to jeopardize our living situation with our uncle. As soon as this happened, my younger brothers were once again hanging out with the drug dealers. They began to skip school because they felt there was no longer any need to maintain their grades. The praise for the God-given talent they possessed had now ceased. They were now flipping for the neighborhood hustlers and friends to get 'hood respect.

After a while, the situation with our uncle began to unravel. Frustration and constant arguments were increasingly common. Finally, my brothers left school and became immersed in the lifestyle of the drug dealer. In a way, it was like watching an experiment. When positive tools and resources are stripped from a child who needs them to grow, other things will inevitably take their place.

When positive tools and resources are stripped from a child who needs them to grow, other things will inevitably take their place.

Within a year, I left my uncle's house and moved in with my grandparents to finish my last year of high school. I started thinking about college and recognized that it would be an opportunity to get away from all the hurt and pain I'd experienced. Given my experiences, intelligence, and even my tribulations, I believed I could be accepted into the top schools in the country. There were only two institutions on my list, Princeton University and Morehouse College.

When I informed one of my guidance counselors that I wanted to attend either Princeton University or Morehouse College, she laughed at me. She said that my high school grades would only allow me to gain acceptance into a community college.

I was a bit hurt by her lack of confidence in my ability. I had already completed the application for Morehouse College, and I was confident that I could get accepted. However, as I walked out of the counselor's office and onto the street, I went to the nearest garbage can and threw in my application. It is funny how most people don't know what they say to an individual can hurt his future or scare him away from his dreams.

14

PARENT &
TEACHER NIGHT

College became more and more a topic of discussion when I was in my senior year of high school. I was involved in many school activities and doing what I could with what I had. It was an exciting time and I wanted to enjoy every last bit of it. I would do things like walk through the halls after school thinking about my first day arriving as a freshman. I would spend time talking with the janitors and lunch aides who served our food everyday. I really enjoyed my time at school because it was my refuge and safe haven. I could be myself and express myself through the friends I made and the work I created as an art major in Arts High (I guess you can see that it was a big deal to me.)

At the time I was working at Planned Parenthood, a nonprofit organization that provides reproductive health services in the United States and internationally. The organization directly provides a variety of reproductive health services and sexual education, contributes to research on reproductive technology, and does advocacy work aimed at protecting and expanding reproductive rights. I was working in the teen program funded by the organization. My boss, the director of the program, was named Maranda. She was a very intelligent, strong-minded, and compassionate woman. She wasn't about to let us make excuses or look for shortcuts (as I am sure many of us do or did in our teenage years from time to time)

One day, I came to work and everyone was talking about Parent and Teacher Night at our high school. Everyone was talking about how their parents would be meeting them at the school and about having them meet their teachers. I, on the other hand, just kept quiet and listened with excitement for them. Maranda asked me if I was also going and I told her that I was. then mentioned that I might not go because my parents aren't around. There was a bit of silence, but it didn't last long enough to make me feel uneasy.

Then she offered to go and play the role of my mother . . . None of my teachers had ever met my mother, so I was sure it would work.

Maranda asked me to stay after work so she could talk to me. When everyone left she asked if I really wanted to go and I gave her a nod with a yes. Then she offered to go and play the role of my mother. She said if that wasn't okay with me, she would accept my decision. But I really wanted her to attend with me, so I agreed. I made her promise not to tell anyone that she wasn't my mother. None of my teachers had ever met my mother, so I was sure it would work.

When we arrived to the school that night, everyone was in awe that my mother showed up. I remember my teacher saying, "This is your mother? She is beautiful." He began flirting with her, which made me laugh. Maranda would look at me and wink as she talked to my teachers and friends. She listened with such appreciation when she heard about the good things I did, and she would give me a real mother's frown when she heard of my playfulness and occasional lack of interest in certain classes.

I was full of excitement and appreciation for what she did. No one knew that Maranda wasn't my biological mother, but at that precise moment, she truly was my mother. We

both walked out of the school with wide smiles. It was love in its purest form. As we stood outside the school, I watched her eyes tear up with gratitude and appreciation for the night. Friends and teachers walked out, saying, "See you on Monday, Rahfeal. Good night, Ms. Gordon."

After that, how could I not believe that people come into your life for a reason or season?

After that, how could I not believe that people come into your life for a reason or season? Maranda played a role in my life on that evening that hadn't been filled for almost four years. My mother didn't come to one parent-teacher night during my high school years, but that final year, she showed up.

The following weeks, Maranda asked me about my plans for after graduation and noticed that I was on the fence about college and where I was going to attend, ever since the negative statement by one of my counselors. So she put on her mother's hat and made me bring every college application I could get my hands on to work. Instead of coming to the teen sessions after school, she directed me to an empty office and had me fill out those applications.

I applied to all the colleges and universities that sounded interesting and well known. I did not have good grades, but I did score well on the SAT. Every time I arrived home at my grandparents' house, we would eagerly waited to see which institution would be my destination. And then it came.

All the doubts that I wasn't going succeed were now irrelevant.

I was accepted to Montclair State University. I yelled and screamed, excited beyond reason. I showed my grandparents the letter, and they hugged me with equal joy. After everything I had experienced, I was going to college. All the doubts that I wasn't going succeed were now irrelevant. I was from the one of toughest parts of Newark, New Jersey, and I was about to be a college student.

The day after I found out, I went by the office where Maranda worked and shared with her the news. It was a blessed moment for me. I was going to college and one of my dear mothers was there to share in the moment with me.

15

TEAM INFINITE
AND THE INVISIBLE FIGHT

As I entered college, I knew I wanted to make an impact. I joined all the organizations I could, and learned what was needed to make possible all the things I wanted. At the same time, I roughly adapted to college life because I didn't know about credit, financial aid, scheduling classes, and all the things that were expected from a freshman. I was accepted into college with the help of the EOF program, which I am so thankful and grateful to be one of their alumni. The Educational Opportunity Fund (EOF) provides financial assistance and support services (e.g. counseling, tutoring, and developmental course work) to students who attend institutions of higher education but come from educationally and economically disadvantaged backgrounds. The lessons counselors taught me and the resources made available to me helped me realize the importance of an education.

I arrived on Montclair State University campus in June 2001. When I moved onto campus a week before I graduated high school to start the EOF program, it was as if I knew that would be my home for the next few years. I felt comfortable and a simultaneous sense that I'd arrived and actually made it out. It was a whole new world (drop the background music to the Disney movie, "Aladdin," please haha).

Once I was settled, I roamed around the campus and stumbled upon the Student Center. I walked around the building and ended up in the Student Activities Department. It was there that I found out about the organizations on the campus. There were so many! I wanted to join and leave my mark on them all. I ended up meeting a woman who was a graduate work student in the department. I asked her so many questions, I knew she was ready to just throw all the pamphlets at me. Then I asked the one question that would set the tone for my entire college life, "Can I start my own organization?" She said, "you sure can!"

Then I asked the one question that would set the tone for my entire college life . . .

My face lit up and before I could fire another million questions, she directed me to the SGA (Student Government Association) where I could get all the information to begin the process during the fall semester. It was there that I met the person who would DJ all my college parties, DJ Reef. He was in his senior year and the current SGA Treasurer. We greeted each other and I started shooting out questions about starting my own organization. Even though I could tell he wasn't that sold on my ideas, he still took the time to provide me all the information I needed to write my proposal and go over the instructions I needed to establish my organization during the fall semester.

One life lesson that sticks with me about this moment is that we all tend to meet people along our journey who have no clue that they are in our path to give us something to continue to fulfill our God-given purpose. Even though I was starting college, I was actually there to meet people who had the tools of insight to help me build something beautiful to inspire the world.

Once I left the SGA office, I headed over to my residence hall and got to work. Every single day, I worked on my organization's articles and proposal for the SGA. I followed the guidelines and made sure I did everything right. I completed the entire plan within a week after meeting DJ Reef. He provided me his contact and told me to reach out anytime I needed help. And call is what I did. We met up and I provided him all the information and showed him the plan. He was shocked and realized that I was truly serious. The organization was to be called, Team Infinite. The mission was to focus on creating campus unity, creating events that amplified school spirit, and develop leaders. We spent a good amount of time reviewing my drafts and making sure I had everything right before I submitted it to the SGA for review and voting in the fall semester to be a chartered organization.

I submitted the documents the first week of the SGA being active in the fall semester. I wasted no time because I just knew it would be the coolest and most popular organization on the campus. Word started getting around the campus about the freshman who submitted a proposal to establish an organization. This wasn't normal to anyone's knowledge in the history of the SGA that a freshman chartered an organization as a freshman in their first semester. There was excitement happening especially amongst the minorities on campus. We were nowhere near the majority of the population at the university. I learned quickly what happens when you start to make change or do something out of the ordinary.

There was a major back to school party on campus hosted by one of the Greek fraternities. It was my very first college and Greek party. I had already started making a name for myself being that I had been at school prior to the fall semester starting. Seeing many of the student leaders and them showing me love, made my first college party experience an epic one. The moment was short lived because a huge fight broke out towards the end of the party, which caused the university to band all Greek or hip hop parties until further notice. It was a major blow for students, especially the freshman class.

The following week, it was the talk of the campus. The crazy fight that lead to the banning of parties in the Student Center. As I was leaving one of my classes, I heard someone softly say, "Excuse me, are you Rahfeal Gordon?" I turned around to notice this slinky white guy with glasses staring at me with a pad and pen.

I told my fellow classmates I would catch up. I responded, "Yeah, that's me. What's going on." I didn't think there was any problem or felt the need to be nervous. Until he stated, "You own Infinite Productions? Is that a business?" I responded with a 'yes' but then something started to feel uncomfortable about the situation. He then proceeded to ask me questions about where I'm from, how much money my business made, and what I planned to do with Team Infinite. I was very confused and started to get angry.

He said, "You can't have a business and an organization." I didn't know this guy. I'd never met him in my life. We were not from the same hood nor shared the same classes. We didn't even have the same friends. I told him, "I don't know why you asking me these questions or approaching me like this. Yo, I'm outta here." He started following while yelling out more questions. I was confused, angry, and felt harassed. It was the first of many incidents I would have with him. He would randomly pop up in the cafeteria and at events I attended as if he knew my schedule. He even popped up and waited for me after a Black Student Organization event. This time, I was with some of my big bros and student leaders. He usually caught me by myself, but this time his heart was pumping sugar. He was scared to approach. I heard nervousness in his tone when he said, "I have a few questions to ask you." You would have thought I was some big-time celebrity or did something so big it was primetime newsworthy. He ended up speeding off once one of my friends, who didn't like what was happening, started to approach him aggressively.

I was confused, angry, and felt harassed. It was the first of many incidents I would have with him.

We found out that he was part of the SGA board and would more than likely become SGA President the following year. He was trying to get as much information on me to block my organization from being chartered. I didn't understand why he wanted to do that. I was just minding my business, trying to be a great leader while in college. My first semester and not even a full month in, and this was happening to me.

I sat around and pondered on what I could do. Some of my friends where presidents of prestigious organization chapters on campus, so I decided to get all of them together and share what happened (some had seen it for themselves). I explained to them that when students joined Team Infinite, they would get a tag to wear around their necks with the mission statement. I immediately gave them all one and told them they were official members. They helped me get the signatures needed prior to my presentation on the day the SGA board had to vote. I wanted to make sure that when I walked into the SGA meeting on voting day, I would have the biggest turn out and student leader power they had ever seen. And that is exactly what happened.

Of course, my hater raised his hand. He went on to explain why I didn't deserve . . .

I walked into the meeting and said hello to everyone, including the SGA member who stalked me for weeks to sabotage that day. When it was my turn to speak, I walked to the front podium and so did the student leaders on campus and those who would be joining as soon as we were chartered. Everyone was wearing their tag and I even passed out tags to every voting SGA member present. Prior to the voting, the SGA President asked if there was anyone who believed Team Infinite didn't deserve to be chartered. Of course, my hater raised his hand. He went on to explain why I didn't deserve to have an organization and how I ran a business off campus, along with other things a true hater would say to block someone's blessing.

At the end, the SGA majority vote was in my favor. I ended up having an active organization on campus my first semester. I went on to charter a second chapter on Bloomfield College's campus with help of a high school friend, Terrance Bankston, who attended there. That chapter became the largest active organization on that campus during my college years.

During the following semester, Montclair State decided to lift the ban and gave Team Infinite the opportunity to host the first college party of the second semester since the ban was put in place. It became the most talked about party all year. We hosted some of the biggest events on campus and raised funds for other organizations on campus for the years I attended Montclair State University.

Team Infinite's mission impacted hundreds of thousands of students within Northern New Jersey. It was and continues to be an organization that represents the next generation of leaders who yearn for the change that so many students want to see in their lifetime.

16

TWO IN,
TWO OUT

My college experience was beautiful despite any learning curves or hardships I had to deal with on campus. I was safe from harm, and I was learning a new game that would transfer into preparing me for adulthood. Even though, I became the first in my immediate family to go to college, I still had to navigate spending great deal away from my loved ones and those who stepped in and took great care of me during the previous years.

I returned to Newark often because I still wanted to see old friends and family. My brothers were still in the hood, and despite my success, I refused to desert them. I remember being in my dorm when I received anonymous phone calls saying I should check on my brothers because they were causing mayhem in the hood. The phone calls caused me much stress, and I didn't know what to do.

I drove to Newark, and as soon as I arrived in the area, I came across an old childhood friend. I probably hadn't seen him in years, and I was surprised by his first words.

"Yo, your two brothers are off the hook. Those two dudes are wild boys. Someone is gonna have to calm them down."

My cousin was in the car and just looked at me when she heard his words. I knew she was wondering what he was referring to, but I didn't want to talk about it.

I took my cousin home, and I began searching for my brothers. I went to where they used to congregate and discovered that they were no longer on that side of the street. When I received updated directions, I immediately drove to the new location. As I approached the house they stayed in, I hopped out of the car and rang the doorbell. Alfonso answered the door, and he hugged me with his huge arms while Isaiah walked out nonchalantly. The three of us talked, and then I pulled Alfonso to the side.

My cousin was in the car and just looked at me when she heard his words.

I told him the situation and what I had heard, and he said he was loose (meaning not caring). But he told me not to worry because he would take care of Isaiah.

"You just do what you gotta do because you're in college. If you need us, you know how to find us."

I believed him. I knew that he would take care of Isaiah and keep him in his place because that's how it always was. Alfonso had Isaiah and I had Janvier. When I needed Janvier, he was there; when Alfonso needed Isaiah, he was there.

Our separate yet complete bond was known as two in, two out. Nobody could understand how the four of us could be so close but so distant in location. We all supported each other, but none of us was ready for the situation that was about to occur.

17

THE PROMISE

One day I decided to visit my uncle and hang out in the old neighborhood. I drove down the Garden State Parkway towards Irvington, New Jersey. When I arrived at my uncle's home, folks in the living room were planning a family reunion that was scheduled for July. I said hello to everyone, and I went to the kitchen for a drink. As I returned from the kitchen, my little brother Alfonso arrived through the front door. I was amazed at how big he had grown and how his dread locks were so long. We greeted each other as warmly as any brothers from the hood would do.

I decided to return to the kitchen to talk to Alfonso. He looked tired and stressed, and I could imagine what my 19 year old brother was experiencing in the hood. He told me that he stashed his clothes in the wall behind a 50 Cent poster and washed his clothes when our uncle wasn't home.

Alfonso then asked me to help him get an apartment, but I quickly declined because I knew it would be with drug money. I told him that he could stay with me, but he insisted that it was too far from where he needed to be. I didn't want to become involved in the street life now, and I felt it would place me in a position where I didn't want or need to be.

Alfonso said he understood my decision and proceeded to walk out the door. I sat down and began eating some food, but it was tasteless. I started to feel as if I should be running out the door to talk to my brother. I knew he was returning to the corner where only two things happened, death and jail. I called him back down the street and expressed how I felt and how I needed him to change.

"You gonna have to be strong because you are going to be representing a lot of people who struggle."

"Hey big bro, if you make it on TV I will leave the street game. I will put everything down only if you call me and tell me you are on TV," Alfonso said.

I could tell he was serious by the tone in his voice.

"You are going to be big bro! But remember that these clowns are gonna hate. You gonna have to be strong because you are going to be representing a lot of people who struggle. They are going to be from the hood and from the top. We need a celebrity who represents the homeless and project babies like us," he continued.

He then said, "You told me to be the best man in whatever I do! And that is what I am going to do, be the best of the street game! Nobody really wants to help me, so I gotta do what I gotta do. They talk a good game, but they not real! You real big bro! You could have been a kingpin out here with all the people you know, but you chose to go to college and sell PARTY tickets rather than the color tops. And I respect you for that."

"Yo, big bro," he continued, "You are harder than most

of these suckers out here. Those dudes you go to school with may never know our struggle, but they will soon from you. But keep that smile with a nation behind you as you tell our story! You gonna be big like Jay-Z and Puffy! I believe in you! I really believe in you!

I continued to listen intently.

"Big bro, I love you! And real talk, as you say, a man's words are weak if his actions are weak. If you make it on television, I will leave the street life alone and do whatever you say."

As my little brother walked up the street, I yelled, "Alfonso, don't go back there!"

"Fuck everybody else Rah! Just do you! But tell our story! If you don't tell our story, you will never be as big as you want to be! So just tell our story."

18

POWER OF
FORGIVENESS

All of my college friends were getting ready to go to Miami for Memorial Day weekend. I wanted to go, but for some reason, I couldn't get myself together. I had never been to Miami while in college, and I made a promise to myself that this would be the year. I had my own apartment, a car, a full course load, and had the parties rocking for the college students. The spring semester was complete, and I was taking two summer courses while working as an intern with Enterprise Rental Car Service. I was doing well, yet I couldn't understand why I couldn't push myself to hang out with the college and local superstars.

My friends, including my roommate, left for Miami to enjoy the weekend festivities on Thursday and Friday while I stayed home. I made Ramen noodles and watched *Law & Order* the entire night. When I decided to go to bed, it was late. As I was getting ready for bed, I felt moody with many emotions, and my mind was in a state of dullness. However, I stilled managed to go to sleep quickly and gracefully.

Suddenly, it was very obvious why I did not go to Miami. I remember this day as if it were yesterday. At 4:23 a.m., I was awakened by a phone call from my cousin. I could hear the stiffness in his voice.

"He's dead Rah! They killed him Rah!" My mind struggled to process the words. "Calm down! Who's dead?" I asked.

As he caught his breath, he replied, "They killed Alfonso."

My heart pounded and I began to cry as I never have cried before. I didn't sleep for days. I planned the funeral with my family. It has and will always be a moment that made me realize that life is full of surprises.

*I*t has and will always be a moment that made me realize that life is full of surprises.

During my brother's funeral, I reflected on my brother's life and even made a statement that this could be the result when a child is not properly cared for. I also said that these situations can make you stronger or weaker. I chose to let it make me stronger.

As time passed, friends, acquaintances, police, and detectives called my family and me to see if we were okay. Additionally, I would stop by where my brother stayed from time to time. Alfonso had received love from many people, and to see that was very important to me.

Two months later, I received a call that the man that murdered my brother was apprehended and in custody. It made me feel good because we had so many people supporting the family to ensure justice was served.

At the same time, I started receiving letters as invitations to court hearings. I attended the listed dates to see justice for my brother's murder. Then I received a letter and a call about confronting the man who took my brother's life. I had so many things running through my head that I didn't know where to begin. I told the caller that I would want to meet him, and the court set a date.

As the date to meet my brother's murderer approached, some of my family discovered my intention to confront him. They advised me that I shouldn't go, but I felt it was necessary. At the time, I was working at the New Jersey Performing Arts Center in Newark. I didn't tell anyone at work what I was going to do on that day because I felt it was something that I had to do to move forward. I took my lunch break, and I headed to the court. When I arrived, I was escorted upstairs and met my grandmother who accompanied me for support. After my grandmother and I spoke for a while, the judge entered and the proceedings commenced.

The minutes seemed to go so quickly yet slowly as I waited for the moment to meet my brother's murderer.

The minutes seemed to go so quickly yet slowly as I waited for the moment to meet my brother's murderer. I had waited for this opportunity for the last two years. As the murderer entered the court room, he looked rough and rugged as though he hadn't slept since the day he was apprehended.

We soon discovered that the murderer was actually on trial for two murders. A family who sat in front of us was also victims of his sin; he had taken the life of their father, brother, son, and husband. Members of this family were the first to express their emotions to him.

Once they finished, I was told that it was my turn to confront my brother's murderer. As I approached the podium, I began to shake as many emotions stirred inside me. When I reached the front of the podium, the man was sitting down. I asked the judge to allow him to stand because I felt he shouldn't deserve to sit while I spoke to him. Once they allowed him to stand, I looked into his eyes and addressed him.

"You know, I have so much I want to say, but I don't think it will do any good. You took a life from this world. You took my brother's life who I loved with all my heart. I could curse you, but why? I just wanted to let you know that I forgive you for taking my brother's life. I truly, truly forgive you. As a godly man, I cannot hate you. I love you from the bottom of my heart. But best believe that you will have long days and longer nights. When you dream, remember my face and name. You have made me a stronger man, and because of your actions, I will become powerful. I pray that you find God while doing your bid and realize your sins. I thank you. I love you. And I forgive you."

I turned away and headed towards my grandmother. I kissed her on the forehead and told her that I was returning to work. As I walked back to work, I knew that my burden was lifted because I was moving as if I were gliding through the air with my wings widely spread.

19

WHAT YOU ARE
SEEKING IS SEEKING YOU

After everything settled down after Alfonso's passing, I decided to leave school the following year. I was into my final year of college, but I was a complete mess. I was no longer interested in what was happening on campus, in my classrooms, with the social life, or with the events I was hosting throughout New Jersey.

Prior to leaving school, I wrote a one-page autobiography. Yes, I really wrote a one-page autobiography. So please hold your laughs—thanks! The document stated who I was, what I'd been through, and what I was willing to do to go to the top.

After I wrote the paper, I was able to have a friend edit it for me. I went to the computer lab on campus and printed about 100 copies. I put each one in a white envelope and sealed them tight. I didn't drive, so I took a bus down to the *Newark Star-Ledger* newspaper building. I stood in front of the building and passed out each envelope to anyone who walked into the building. I was determined to have someone read or know my story. Security came outside and had me move away from the entrance, so I just walked to the side of the building and kept handing out those envelopes containing my one-page biography. I stood outside for hours until I had no more envelopes to hand out.

Nothing happened on that day. Not one person ran downstairs and said "your story is powerful." Not one person offered to drive me anywhere. Not one person offered to helped me pass out those envelopes outside in the cold. But that's how it is when you are trying to do the unthinkable, unimaginable, and extraordinary.

I remember calling one of my friends on the phone, upset. I'd had high hopes that someone would hear my cry or my call for help. I was seeking a way out of the pain, suffering, and looking for a way to heal the wounds that were invisible but deep. But even during my attempt to knock on the doors of the *Star-Ledger*, I had no clue that what I was searching for was actually seeking me.

. . . I had no clue that what I was searching for was actually seeking me.

As things were getting more hectic in my internal world, I had a feeling that something inside of me wanted to come out. I needed to get away to clear my mind, so I went to the home of one of my college friends. She always gave me a shoulder when I needed to talk. I explained to her all that was happening and she reconfirmed that things would get better. Just trust that God will provide was her message to me in so many ways.

As she went off to the kitchen to cook, I began watching *MTV Jams* with the volume muted. *MTV Jams* is a show that airs on the Music Television Video network that shows the most popular music videos in hip hop. I noticed that all they were showing was half- naked women, jewelry, cars, and as much violence that your brain can absorb through your eyes. I began yelling to my homegirl about what I was seeing on TV. I then asked myself, what if I could change the game in hip hop? What if, instead of being a rapper, I could be a motivational speaker in the hip hop world.

I then had the craziest idea:

What if I could be a motivational speaker who is as cool as Jay Z but as brilliant in business as a Bill Gates or Warren Buffett?

I then had the craziest idea: What if I could be a motivational speaker . . .

I said to my friend, "I want to inspire people to do big things and be great in life. Most of these dudes on television are actors; they don't know half this stuff. But what if I actually live a great life and I can actually teach and show people how to do it!?"

She thought it was a great idea and even said, "But you are already inspiring many people, Rah. You just don't see it all the time 'cause you are being you. I think that fits you perfectly. You should do it."

I pondered the idea as I went home, but I didn't feel it was the right time; I was still building up the courage to leave school.

When I finally made the decision, I attended my final class before actually leaving; it with my late mentor, Dr. Susan Weston. I adored her because she was always honest with me and gave it to me straight. As I was leaving her class, she pulled me aside in the hallway and said, "I know you are going to pursue your personal goals and dreams and may just accomplish them all, but don't that get in the way of your education. You have to finish what you started. In this world, as a young African-American man, coming from what you've come from, you must finish. I'm a old Jewish woman telling you that you must finish your education, Rahfeal."

I truly adored Dr. Weston for pushing me to be more and do more. I told her I would definitely come back, but I had to pursue what my gut was telling me. Once I left, I had much more time on my hands. And that's when I started contemplating the idea of being a motivational speaker. The next and final chapter you are about to read will show you how the universe works and helps you find all that you seek.

20

THE
GREAT ESCAPE

I went for every opportunity during my time away from school. I did not leave a single stone unturned. I didn't want to live with regret about leaving school and not giving my all to my dreams and goals. I told a close friend that I could only rely on my faith and actions now. I didn't have the luxury of relying on my college degree, because I don't have one.

Things began to move along slowly. Nevertheless, progress was being made. I networked with everyone at every event I attended. I attended as many seminars, conferences, and workshops as I could with the free time I had. If I was going to nightclub events with friends, I would bring a book in my back pocket. You could catch me in VIP among people popping bottles, highlighting a sentence in *Think and Grow Rich* by Napoleon Hill. I was not playing any games. It was all or nothing.

At a certain point, I realized I needed to come up with a title for my seminar. I settled on, "Hip Hop Saved My Life." I broke the story of my life into three parts like three verses of a hip hop song. I waned to show the world that I was hip hop and you could tell your story even if you didn't want to be a rapper. It was difficult getting this across to people in the beginning. Everything I was doing screamed, "Bro, just be a rapper." But, I wanted to be the biggest motivational, hip hop speaker on the planet. I even thought that if I could make history as the first signed motivational speaker to a record label, it would be huge!

That became my mission for the following months, to be signed to a record label. And what better record label than Def Jam, which Shawn "Jay-Z" Carter was the President of. Now, I know what you are thinking. You have to realize that I was trying to do something that I had never seen done before. And I didn't want to be like everyone else. I wanted to make a name for myself and impact the world in the coolest way possible.

I created a Hip Hop Saved My Life business plan and various promotional materials to hand out with the business plan. Some people weren't impressed, while others questioned if I dropped out of college to be a rapper. It was another one of those moments where people just don't see what you see clearly. I knew I was onto something; I could only describe it based upon what I was exposed to. Once I had my pitch package completed, I started promoting myself all over New Jersey and New York City. I was even able to have the Montclair State University SGA pay me close to $3,800 to perform Hip Hop Saved My Life seminar for my former class and professors.

And how about the fact that the student who stalked me during my freshman year was the President of the SGA and didn't hesitate to sign off on the proposal and have the treasurer cut me a check.

I was onto something big! After making the front page of my college newspaper, I just knew I had to move fast. A friend of mine thought I should try to get signed to a label even if it sounded farfetched. I wasted no time heading to New York City to give out my business plans to everyone who exited out of Def Jam's office building. The same way I did in front of the *Newark Star Ledger New Paper* headquarters.

I commuted to New York City early in the morning looking for the building that housed Def Jam's offices. I decided to bring 50 business plans to give out to those who came through the doors that looked like they worked in the music business. As luck would have it, the security guard advised that there was no soliciting in front of the building. Although I was at the right building, it didn't mean I would be able to just walk into the offices without an appointment with someone. I was not discouraged. I was simply not aware of the security regulations for the building. I thought to myself I could do one of two things, I could leave the building and go somewhere else or I could sit in front of the building as motivation to figure out how to get everyone in the right offices to know me. I decided to stay because something inside me said, *"What do you have to lose? The only place to go is up!"*

Once I had my mental discussion, I pulled out a mini-pad and started reevaluating my strategy while sitting right in front of the building. An hour passed and I was in my grinding zone. I was thinking and planning while looking up at the building for motivation, and then writing my ideas on my mini-pad.

I watched unsigned artists rush up to everyone who came outside the door. Most were rappers with a few singers sprinkled around the area. Everyone was plotting to get signed. I watched as singers walked directly up to people and just sang. I watched rappers just bust out spitting their lyrics to anyone who looked like they worked for the label. I had never seen that before. It was a different type of hunger. It was a different type of grind.

I sat there trying to figure out what would be my line. What would be my pitch because I definitely wasn't aiming to be a rapper. Still, I had the focus and hunger to make things happen. While sitting there, I started talking to a guy from Virginia. He and I ended up sitting next to each other sharing our goals and aspiration of wanting to make it. He was sleeping in his car after driving to New York from Virginia close to a week prior. All he was doing was writing in his note pad, pitching everyday in front of the building and sleeping in his car. He was determined to get a deal. He was completely serious when he said, "I'm not going back to Virginia. I'm going to make it."

After awhile, I began to hear my stomach growl. It was time to eat, and the summer heat was telling me it was time to go. I was done. I tried and nothing turned out in my favor. So, I told my Virginia buddy I was heading out and wished him all the best. I figured I could head over to the BET Networks office to see if my friends over there could give me some assistance. I was hesitant at first because what if I got a chance to meet Jay-Z? What if I was able to get signed and my idea was something that caught an executive's attention?

As I started walking away with my bookbag and business plans in hand, I could hear a voice inside of me scream, "Noooo don't go! Stay!" My entire body was feeling the emotion of something greater than me, pulling me to stay. I stopped for a second and looked back at where I was sitting. Then at that moment, a lesson was gifted to me . . .

A Maybach pulled up in front of the Def Jam building. I mean it pulled up directly in front of where I was sitting prior to me getting up. I couldn't believe it! I said to myself, *That's gotta be Jay-Z. Who else could it be?*

The curtains in the backseat of the car were closed. I couldn't see who they were hiding. I stayed put and watched as the front car door opened. A fair skin brother jumped out of the right side of the back seat. Ten seconds later, the driver opened the left side and out stepped Jay-Z. The man I grew up listening to. The person who changed a culture trend with one video. He moved a nation with a freestyle. A person who motivated me in business by his lyrics, "*9–5 is how you survive, but I'm not tryin' to survive, I'm trying to live it to the limit and love it a lot!*"

I said to myself, *I have finally seen Jay-Z in the flesh. I'm satisfied, now I'm leaving.*

But then I said to myself, *NO! I have an idea! A great, big lifesaving idea! I know he will support it if I present it to him!*

So, I said to myself, "*Rahfeal, go now and speak to him. Represent the thousands of people who struggle to find opportunities that will help them make their dreams come true. Even if it doesn't work out, at least you can be content knowing you tried and you don't have to live with regrets.*"

As I approached Jay and the guy who was in the car with him, one of the young rappers pushed past me running over to Jay and said, "Yo, Jay give me a shot. I'm hot. I got a crazy buzz. I am shuttin' Brooklyn down right now. What's up? I am hot, son!"

I was mad. First, this guy pushed past me and didn't say excuse me. Secondly, he was jeopardizing my opportunity because it looked like we were together waiting for Jay-Z.

Fortunately, Jay seemed to notice that we weren't together. Maybe it was the dude's appearance or maybe it was his begirting approach. Who knows how Jay-Z recognized our differences. My big lesson that day was one that would continue to fuel me to reach for stadium status. I walked over to Jay-Z's friend and said, "I have this idea. Could you give my package to Jay because the dude over there is taking up too much of Jay's time and I know both of you value your time."

I said this to him because when you are around someone important, you have to make sure you provide something that is equally important for the time you are asking for. I explained my project to him, just to give him some background of what was in my package. He told me that he thought the idea was amazing but they are not allowed to take unsolicited packages. He told me to contact a specific person who one of the heads of A&R at that time. He told me to make an appointment to present my project and provided some insight on how to do that. As our conversation ended, I turned and walked over to hear the conversation between Jay-Z and ambitious young rapper. The young rapper kept talking. I caught Jay-Z's eye to let him know I was recognizing the dudes "all talk, no proof" conversation. Then Jay started teaching. "Let me show you something," Jay said to the young rapper.

Jay had the young rapper physically switch places with him on the sidewalk. Then Jay said to him, "If you were in my position and I came to you in your position right now and said, 'Yo, I'm Jay-Z. I am the hottest rapper out of Brooklyn,' would you believe me?"

The young rapper said, "Yea, I'd believe you!"

Jay replied, "No you wouldn't. The only reason you are saying you would believe me is because you know me as Jay-Z right now."

At that point, Jay glanced at me as I nodded my head in agreement with what he said. He then said, "You gotta be heard before I see you. How are you going to say you are the hottest rapper in Brooklyn and I'm from Brooklyn? What makes you think I don't know what goes on in my borough? If you are hot, where is your following? Where is your press package? Why don't you have a shirt that promotes who you are? Why didn't you offer to spit a rhyme? You must understand that you gotta have movement so people can hear you. So, when you come to present yourself to me, you present yourself with your city behind you." (Please Note: I am generalizing this conversation with the intent to give you a positive understanding of what he was teaching us).

He went on to say that you must always take care home and build your fan base at home first because if you leave your hood and it don't work out at first, you can always come back home and start again within your city. They will be your safety net to help build you back up to try again.

While Jay-Z spoke, I was mentally taking notes of all the jewels he dropped in my head—the knowledge, the wisdom, the understanding. I looked down at my package and said to myself, *I'm not ready yet.*

Although I did not present myself as a rapper, I still learned from all the points he was making to the young rapper. After a few minutes, the young rapper left. Jay then approached me. All I could do was put my hand over my heart and say softly, "I pay homage to you. I'll see you soon."

He nodded, shook my hand, and walked into the building. The man that was with him looked at me for the last time and told me to make that call and to keep pushing because I got something worthwhile. All I could say to him was, "Thank you," and proceeded to the BET offices to share what happened.

I started gaining more momentum after that day. I was pumped and motivated. One day, I received a call from a friend who worked at BET, Eric. I always appreciated Eric for showing me love and support with the things I was creating on our campus at Montclair State University. He called to inform me that BET was having an audition for a show about college event planner/promoters. He thought it would be perfect for me. The catch was I had to submit my own audition tape via mail within the next two days. I didn't have a video camera and I didn't have anyone to film me. That didn't matter. I used every resource I could to get it done.

This is how I did it . . .

- I was able to get a camcorder from a college friend.

- I set up in a conference room in downtown Newark that I paid for monthly through a virtual office service.

- I didn't have anyone to help film me, so I emptied the trash out of the conference room trashcan, placed the can upside down, and put the camcorder on top.

- The TV producers called me to ask their interview questions and I was able to film myself while answering.

- The next day, I sent the tapes out by next-day service and they had the tapes on the day of the deadline.

After a few weeks of waiting, I received a call telling me that I had been cast for the new television show. I was ecstatic. I celebrated with friends; things were on the way up for me. I was flown to Los Angeles to prepare for show. While in Los Angeles, I went to the L.A. Convention Center, where there was a business expo going on. I met a young woman named Tove who worked for a magazine company called *Black Enterprise*. We exchanged contact information and stayed in touch during the period of my TV development.

But, things never go quite as planned. When I returned home, I spent time with friends and family. I went to a park with a close friend to play basketball and ended up tearing my Achilles tendon. Because I wasn't able to walk, I couldn't continue on the TV show. I went into a deep depressive state.

I lost the television show, dropped out of college, had no money from my event planning business, and I was back in the 'hood thinking there was no way out.

God works in mysterious ways . . .

I was still in contact with Tova. She suggested that I pick back up the idea I'd had about becoming this new-generation speaker. She was starting a publishing company and thought it would be cool if I was her first client. Every day I wrote a page for my book. It was a short book, but it was *my* short book. Once Tova read it, she said something was missing. She said I needed to tell my story. With her advice, I ended up writing two short pages and the introduction to the book.

I decided to rent one of the theater rooms inside the New Jersey Performing Arts Theater (NJPAC). The reason why I chose NJPAC was because it was in my hometown. I was able to come up with the funding with the support of my grandparents, friends, relatives, and churches I attended. The sold-out event was held on Thursday, September 21, 2007.

Tova wasn't able to publish and market my book the way I wanted before my show at NJPAC. However, what she did for me in spite of the failed project was an extraordinary blessing. She helped me establish and invest in creating my own publishing company (RahGor Publishing & Co.) with book distribution serving more than 39,000 retailers, libraries, schools, internet commerce companies, and other channel partners.

In the midst of all this, I was able to connect with an editor from the *Star-Ledger* who, two years prior, had written a story on Alfonso and his brothers. The journalist passed me along to another writer named Carrie, who interviewed me multiple times at the same cafe in downtown Newark (I had handwritten my first book at that same cafe). Once she finished, the only thing left was receiving a call about when the article would come out.

My event was in September 2007. The interviews were conducted in October and November of 2007, the publishing company was finalized in December 2007, and on February 3, 2008 . . . I was on the front page of the *Newark Star-Ledger* newspaper.

And that's when I knew . . . *my location was not my destination.*

21

MY LOCATION WAS
NOT MY DESTINATION

After my article came out on the front page of the *Star-Ledger* paper, my spotlight got bigger than I expected. I started receiving hundreds of letters from students from various schools. Teachers were creating projects and lesson plans using my article. My younger brother, who was incarnated at the time, told me inmates were reading the article in prison. It was everywhere and everyone was trying to reach me. It was surreal! I was happy that I was finally being heard and touching people in a positive way.

I was on a train into New York City after the article was released and I noticed a young woman constantly staring at me. At first, I thought nothing of it. After about 15 minutes of realizing she was locked-in on me, I just didn't know what to think. The train arrived at my stop, and I got off to proceed to the street level. Once I got to street level, I started walking fast to make it to my appointment on time.

As I was walking, I heard a young female voice say, "Rahfeal." I turned back and it was the young girl from the train. I stopped and waited for her. When she got close to me, she just stopped and stared at me. She just stared at me. I asked her, "*Uhh*, yes?"

She said with the softest tone, "You're Rahfeal. I saw your article and saw you on the news." She started tearing up and told me I was an inspiration for her. Then she just smiled and walked back down the street. For weeks, I had moments like that with random people within the Tri-State Area. It became overwhelming even though I was very appreciative of everything I was being blessed with.

While all this was happening, I was able to meet with my college counselors and advisors to come up with a plan to finish school. All I needed was a few classes to complete one semester. And finish I did! I even got nominated for an NAACP Image Award with my dear friend, Michael B. Jordan. It was a crazy moment for me. Every single day, I woke up to a new opportunity, idea, request, phone call, invitation, news appearance, etc. It was overwhelming but it was what I asked for. It was what I prayed for, and I knew that for the rest of my life, I could not turn back. I can only and I mean ONLY move forward and fly HIGHER.

When Success Takes a Shot At You

You know, we always focus on reaching success or achieving the goal. We never think about what comes with it. What and who is attached to the light in which you want to sit under after all has been accomplished. I thought I was doing a good thing. I thought all my friends and family would be proud that I was making it out here on my own in the best way I knew how. Was I perfect? NO! Did I make mistakes along the way? YES! I was just trying to survive past the age of 25 in an environment that many young men who look like me do not.

Just as much as I was receiving applause from those who connected to my pain and my drive to want something better, I definitely received my share of pushback and looks of disgust from those who believed I shouldn't have told my story. Some told me to my face while others told it to my brothers and friends. I heard the whispers louder from those who I called family and friends. I had seen the expression on their faces. I had seen the empty reserved seats at the events I had invited them to and they never showed up. The books they didn't want to pay for but believed they deserved for free. It was hard for me to swallow. I started questioning my walk and the decision to tell my story, my truth. Should I have kept it to myself? Should I have just suffered in silence?

I had seen the empty reserved seats at the events I had invited them to and they never showed up.

I started losing friends and close bonds with many people I loved. There was a lot to process. There were times I just wanted to go away and scream, but I kept on going. There were times I cried while speaking on stage. There were moments I was in deep conversations with people as my eyes watered telling my story constantly to inspire those dealing with similar pain. I pushed through over time. I started making new friends and gaining new mentors who asked me questions different than the ones I was used to. I was able to get invited to places to just relax without being required to talk about my personal story. And what's interesting is that it was what I was needed so much when everything was happening so fast.

RahGor Goes Global

As time progressed, I joined various organizations and became the headline speaker for many organizations across the United States. I networked with numerous people on Wall Street, as well as at corporations and universities. I spoke alongside celebrities, athletes, and Fortune 500 executives. I was constantly reordering my book for schools that would make big orders for after-school programs and summer school. It was a blessing; I was finally seeing the fruits of my labor. Of course, we all know that at some point God will let you know that He isn't done with you yet. There is always more to see and experience.

One day, I was on Facebook and a friend of mine posted he was heading to one of his homes in Omaha, Nebraska to attend a Berkshire Hathaway shareholders' meeting. He had a few extra guest passes and was checking to see if anyone wanted to go with him. I told him I would love to and just like that my pass was reserved. I flew in and was blown away that my friend lived around the corner from Warren Buffet, the richest man in American at the time. I walked the neighborhood every day while I was there. I enjoyed meeting all my friend's friends and attending the shareholders' meeting. I was taking notes like crazy every time Warren spoke. There were so many gems and life lessons I learned while in Omaha. It was truly a moment of thinking, "Bro, you from Newark. How the hell did you get here?"

Prior to leaving, I was in the car and my friend said, "Bro, have you spoken out of the country yet?"

I responded, "I haven't yet. I would love to, but I don't know how to do that."

He shared that there was a huge conference in Monterrey, Mexico where he spoke routinely. He was going to be speaking there during the fall and would love to make the introduction to have me speak as one of the headline speakers. I was speechless, excited, and overwhelmed. I told him I would love that and would send over whatever he needed.

I was finally going to use my passport for the first time . . .

A few weeks after my trip to Omaha, I received an email with an invitation to Monterrey, Mexico. I totally couldn't believe it! I was beyond happy. It was too good to be true. I was finally going to use my passport for the first time and take a trip out of the country to tell my story and share my insight about achieving your biggest goal. That feeling is still with me today as I am thinking about all the things that got me to that point.

I sent over all that was requested as I began to prepare for the trip months in advance. Even with all the excitement, a rush of nervousness and fear came over me. It was something I never felt before. How was I excited to go but so scared? It was because all I'd seen on television and movies in my country. As old as I was, I was very nervous. Some of my friends were telling me to be careful and sharing their thoughts of what could happen or what they'd heard. I even went online and saw that the threat for traveling to Mexico was at it's highest alert. I didn't share my fear with anyone, I just said I am going to get through these thoughts and still go. As the days got closer, I got more nervous and excited. Finally, the day came when it was time for me to leave.

You Are Exotic Down Here

When I arrived to Monterrey, I felt the heat and the Latin vibe of the people as soon as I landed. Two college students, who were my hosts while in Monterrey, greeted me. Since my arrival, we have been connected and are friends to this day. I was shown around the city and met with other speakers once I arrived at my hotel. I felt at home, like they were my family. I felt love and a sense of appreciation for who I am and what I was doing in the world.

When I arrived to Monterrey, I felt the heat and the Latin vibe of the people . . .

On the day of my seminar, every attendee received my *Newark Star-Ledger* article and picture that I would autograph. I was excited for every moment while there. I had plenty of time to relax before it was my turn to speak. I took that time to greet students and ask where they were from. Everywhere I went, students ran up to me or formed mini crowds in the hallway just to hear what insight I wanted the world to know, especially our generation.

Time passed and it was just a few minutes left before my turn to speak. I stood in the back of the room to see the hundreds of students and leaders within Monterrey sit excited to hear the next speaker. Right before I went up, I was introduced to the translator who would be in a small area translating my speech to those wearing headphones in the audience.

And then I was being announced to the stage, which at that moment would turn me into an international speaker and leader for the rest of my life.

"Welcome to the stage, Rahfeal 'RahGor' Gordon!!" said the moderator. I yelled on the microphone for everyone to stand up, make a lot of noise and gave hi-fives until I stood on the stage. And they all did. It was electrifying! It was intense! It was a moment that I will never forget!

After my speech, so many people ran up to me for hugs, autographs, and tears. Even the translator was in tears as he shook my hand. I felt honored and a sense of purpose to make people feel this way. I was thankful and spiritually full. I had to step out the room just to take a walk and collect my thoughts. I was in a different headspace than I was before I flew into Mexico. All that fear I had was completely gone. They connected with me. They understood my emotions. And they had seen themselves in me. My mind was fully processing so much at one time.

I went for a walk in a nearby park once I was done speaking and meeting everyone at the conference. There was a VIP dinner that night, but for the rest of the day, we were allowed personal time. I decided to sit on the park bench and observe my surroundings. It was so beautiful to sit and just be still in a new country. I thought about all I'd done over the years just to get to that exact moment. Then something special happened. I heard a sound I have never heard before. It sounded so beautiful. It was sharp but soft and yet so beautiful how it cut through the various noises of the city. I looked around but couldn't grasp where it was coming from. And then a small little black bird flew across my path making the sound. Many other birds started doing the same thing. I had never seen a bird or heard a sound like it before in my life. It was like a child seeing colors or hearing morning bird chirps for the first time. I was learning and being born all over again. All do to me following my dream of wanting to impact and inspire the world.

That evening, we had a beautiful dinner with some very prominent leaders and businesspeople within the city. And then we were all asked if we were ready to party in Mexico. Heck yeah! I work hard and play harder baby! We were told that we would be heading to San Pedro where all the exclusive nightclubs and restaurants are located. I was excited to see another part of the city and country.

Prior to heading out after changing clothes, one of the guys pulled me aside and said, "You know RahGor, you are considered exotic down here."

I replied, "Exotic? Who me? I don't understand."

He and the rest of the guys who were coming out all agreed with smiles. "Yeah, it's not every day you see a black man or black American with an American accent around here. We are going to get into every night club with you," he continued. It was a genuine comment and I totally understood what they all were saying. I just felt different coming from where I'm from and not having images of black men being shown. I felt beyond appreciated and loved in a way that I wasn't used to receiving.

When we arrived into San Pedro, we had a ball from the time we all hopped out of the car. They treated me and created an experience like I was a rockstar! It was incredible. I was on the dancefloor doing my 2-step while the guys I was with told the ladies they liked that I was RahGor from America. They kept asking me to say something, anything in my American accent to the ladies. Maaan, we had so much fun.

Can I Say It Just One Time

As we were hanging out, I was approached by some guys who wanted to take a picture. I said 'no problem'. As I took pictures on the dancefloor, there was a section behind me with one of the top promoters in the city. Everyone was just having a great time. I was introduced and asked if I would like to be in his section. I showed love to all of them.

I was 2 seconds from choking him up while live on Facebook.

Before I did, one of the guys from the dancefloor pulled me and said, "Hey RahGor. Can I say it one time?" I squinted and didn't understand what he was saying or what he meant. The music was loud and we on a crowded dancefloor. People were pulling me from every which way to take selfies. This young guy was excited and he kept saying, "Yo bro! Can I say it one time?" I was trying to understand what he meant.

I said, "Sure."

He pulled out his phone, tapped his Facebook LIVE button, and said, "Yooo! I'm here in with my nigga, RahGor, from America!" Man, you should have seen my face! I was looking at the phone and then looking back at him. I was 2 seconds from choking him up while live on Facebook.

I guess from the look on my face as I pierced through his soul, he got the message. He realized quickly what was happening and quickly apologized. I couldn't let that moment ruin or deter me from all the positive things happening. So, I hopped back into the section and enjoyed the rest of the vibes with the cool kids of Monterrey.

As my final hours were coming to a close in Monterrey, after falling asleep under the bed from partying so hard— haha, I prayed to God with gratitude for all He had allowed me to experience in Mexico. The people were so beautiful and welcoming. There were so many things I learned while in Monterey that debunked many of the opinions, beliefs, and things I was taught about the culture and people of Mexico. I knew I wanted more of these feelings and experiences. As I said my goodbyes and gave hugs to all those who hosted me and took great care of me while on the trip, I told them I would be back and I was their brother. I knew without a doubt they all were my brothers and sisters.

22

THE
GENIUS STRATEGY

After my trip to Mexico, I was completely thinking and moving differently. I stopped going to certain places and entertaining people who didn't want to move on a higher level like me. I needed new mentors and advisors to help me expand my reach across the world. Every single day, I was in front of the computer, networking with everyone I met in Mexico and other international organizations I realized I was somewhat affiliated with. As I was doing this, I had a crazy idea. I wondered what would happen if I pitched to only international organizations, schools, and businesses. I made traction in the U.S. but I felt it wasn't enough. I also started seeing that everyone wanted to be a motivational speaker. I wanted to inspire leaders and entrepreneurs around the world. I wanted prime ministers and presidents to ask me for advice or be motivated by the speeches I gave. I wanted top businessmen and women to book me to headline their company conferences. I wanted children in villages, schools, and places around the world to be empowered. I wanted to be the Bruce Wayne and Batman for Humanity. A superhero. A real life superhero!

So, I decided that for the next 7 days, I would use Facebook and Google to search for every organization, business, school, program, conference to pitch my speaking services and books. I would wake up at around 5:00 a.m. (sometimes 4:00 a.m.) and search until 12 midnight. I made a list of every potential client. I'd focus on the continent, then list the countries I wanted to go to, followed by specific cities. Once I did this, I started on Facebook with typing in "Entrepreneurship conference in Europe" and from there I would be off into my research. I probably pitched to about 100 different institutions, organizations, and businesses combined.

Some responded to let me know they were interested while others just kept my information on file. I received recommendations and I also received responses of disinterest as well. I received a few fake emails that were just trying to steal my identity. I really thought I was going to Africa at one point until they started asking for my social security card along with my passport.

I enjoyed the process of researching and seeing what was out in the world that I could connect to as a young leader and entrepreneur. Every single day, I woke up with a sense of purpose thinking of all the surprises and blessings that were waiting for me. I answered every call back, email, and did whatever was asked just to get one step closer to another opportunity to see another part of the world and empower those within it.

I never let up within my progress to make a connection with someone. I just kept at it with faith that my actions of staying the course and working the plan, I would eventually achieve the goal. And one day, I actually did. I received a message from Kristian Aartun, from Norway, who I had sent my information to. He messaged me on Facebook and via email. He wanted to invite me to the Norwegian International Entrepreneurship Conference and I was ecstatic. We kept in touch during his months of planning, and he kept his word. When I received an official invitation to the event, I had the same feeling of excitement as I did when I was headed to Mexico.

I started sharing the news with my friends and family who were just as excited. It seemed a bit strange to some of my friends to be honest. I remember hearing, "Norway? Where is that?" or, "The same place where the Nobel Peace Prize Ceremony is held?" It was funny to hear all the conversations because it wasn't normal to see a young black man being invited to various countries *. . . you can dream big and see it despite your reality.* or even pushing constantly to headline international events as a speaker. I was breaking down belief systems around men and showing others that you can dream big and see it despite your reality. I was doing it and I wasn't stopping.

When I arrived in Norway, I was blown away by the hospitality and overall experience of Oslo. I bonded with many people who attended the conference. I saw my picture on the mini billboard in the Diellote building as I arrived to speak. It was truly an incredible experience. My friend and brother, Kristian, rolled out the red carpet for all the speakers. Everything from my business accommodations with KLM airlines, BMW drivers, and 5- star hotel stay. I was truly shocked by how I was being treated.

After the conference, we were invited to a dinner at a Pakistani restaurant in Oslo. It would be my first-time eating food of the culture. It was amazing and I met so many incredible people who came to honor us. Before I left, I thanked Kristian a million times and told him I would keep in contact. And that, I did! You would have thought I found my long-lost best friend or brother because since that time, we have been very good friends.

When I arrived back home, I shared the news with everyone. I shared every detail and every emotion I experienced while there. I was sharing my experiences online and it was starting to catch the attention of educators and business leaders. I started to notice that when I arrived back from an international trip, I would have more requests to speak in the states. Authors who had publishing deals questioned how I was able to do this. It became less about my story and more about my business moves. I didn't ignore this one bit.

I still felt I wasn't done with Norway. Something in my spirit was pulling me to go back sooner than later. I arrived back from Oslo in November, and I was trying to go right back. I didn't have anything pending that would send me back until a light bulb went off in my head and I realized something I could do and be part of.

23

THE NOBEL
PEACE PRIZE CEREMONY

The bulb that went off in my head was the thought about attending the Nobel Peace Prize Ceremony. It was always talked about in school because the youngest recipient at that time was still Dr. Martin L. King Jr. Growing up, Oslo and the ceremony seemed like a far off place where people who had Harry Potter special power would go. We never saw it on television and I couldn't tell you the last three people who received it from memory. However, I knew it was one of the most important ceremonies in the world. I knew those who attended and received the award were part of world history. It was a moment where people witnessed and honored those who sacrificed their lives for the greater good of people in their country and humanity as a whole.

On November 16, 2014 at 5:52 a.m. EST, I sent an email to my dear friend and Oslo dinner host, Aamir.

"Good Day Aamir,

Hope you are in great spirits and smiling! Remember, we made a promise!

Quick Question: Is the Noble Peace Prize Ceremony open to the public (tickets/invitations available)?

It has always been my hope to one day attend this phenomenal event(s) to not only be inspired but to take part of a historical moment that recognizes individuals who are changing the world.

I thought that you would be the best person to ask about it."

At exactly, 7:08 a.m. EST, he responded, "I will invite you. I will send you with all the program soon."

I just stared at the screen and shock. *Wait. Huh? Did I read this right? He must haven't read my email correctly!* I thought. There couldn't be any way his response would be exactly what I was hoping for and that swift. It was all true. By the time I had lunch, I received an invitation to a private dinner with Malala Yousafzai and her family the night before she received the Nobel Peace Prize.

I immediately booked my flight and decided to reserve an Airbnb so this time I could embrace living as Norwegians and get an even more authentic feel and appreciation for the city and people.

I arrived to Oslo a day before the dinner. I checked into my Airbnb and unpacked. It was already evening, so I had time to relax and catch up on rest. It was so exciting to be back to a place that over the years would become one of my homes away from home.

The next day, I went sight-seeing and met up with some good people who I met the first time I was in Oslo. Everyone was excited and happy to have me back. They were even more thrilled and excited that I was attending the Nobel Ceremony in honor of Malala Yousafzai and Kailash

Satyarthi. As timed passed, I headed back to my Airbnb to get ready for the dinner.

When I arrived, I was greeted by my friend Aamir who was so happy to see me. He introduced me to a few people and then hurried away to prepare for the arrival of Malalah and her family. Once our special guest arrived, I walked over near the entrance and admired a young girl whose life had become a symbol of change, peace, and purpose bigger than her. We all gathered around the table and listened to my brother, Aamir, give his introductions and kind remarks. He went around the table and introduced everyone and then proceeded to give Malala the floor. As she stood next to her dad and the former Prime Minster of Pakistan, I listened as she inspired us all with her dinner speech, ended with the following statement, "Thank you all for joining us. Such a big step we are taking to make education a top priority. We are standing for the rights of children. It's not just a dinner. We are here for a cause. We want to see quality education for every child."

I started to realize I was scratching the surface of something bigger than myself.

It was powerful, another moment that reminded me to keep going. I started to realize I was scratching the surface of something bigger than myself. Something bigger than what I thought when I was younger standing outside handing out my one-page biography in Newark. Bigger than the awards I was receiving. It was bigger than making a name for myself. It was about representing all those who were trying to make it out of a struggle. It was about all those around the world who didn't have a voice and needed someone to represent for them. To show others what real education and the pursuit of a dream really look like. What leadership for the next generation looks like. I understood all this on that night. I saw everything so clearly and vividly.

The Day of Peace

After dinner, we all took pictures, and I had great conversation with other guests who were vising from other countries as well. The following day, I woke very early because I didn't know if there would be a line outside. I didn't know if there would be crowds and a difficult time trying to access. I arrived outside around 7 a.m. and I was the only one outside. I was probably the only one outside that early except those who had to open up their shops!

I went to a nearby café to have some breakfast and tea. As time passed, I started to see a small group forming. I went over to wait in line. I walked in after being checked and headed to the second level of the building where I would be watching the entire ceremony. And what a ceremony it was. I took plenty of pictures and did a lot of recording. I took a pile of ceremony programs and gifted them to my family during Christmas. I mean, who do you know that goes to the Nobel Peace Prize ceremony and can get the entire speech of someone winning the Nobel Peace Prize every year? This was a once in a lifetime moment for me and I wanted to bring something back to my family.

How Did You Get Here

I watched as the young girl who I met the night before became the youngest receipt of the Nobel Peace Prize. I watched as Malala and Kailash gave their speeches that would echo in the history books for generations to come. Following the ceremony, I was invited to a private dinner with some of her family members, friends, Malala Fund staff, and leadership from of the Nobel Institute.

I arrived to dinner by myself as normal. When I walked into the room, there were a few seats open and a young woman, who had already seen me from afar, signaled for me to sit next to her. We briefly said 'hello' and watched as others walked into the room. I recognized a few people who I waved to, as well as got up to hug with great enthusiasm. Malala was at the official Nobel dinner, and we all were in great spirits for her and way the day met.

After my last greeting and hug to a new dinner guest arrival, I sat back down and looked towards the podium as they prepared for the dinner guest speaker. The young woman next to me tapped me on the leg to have a conversation. I could never forget her words because it was genuine and held no malice. She proceeded to say, "I don't mean to be nosey, but who are you and what do you do?" After a pause, she continued, "Please don't take this the wrong way, but how did you get here?" That would be a question I get asked a lot in places and rooms throughout my journey. She went on to clarify that in all of her work and travels, she barely (and I mean barely) sees a black man, specifically a black American man, in rooms and events such as this. She was honest and sincere. She was authentic and I respected her for all of it. She went on to say, "Whoever you are and what you do is very important whether you know it or not."

It was the statement that validated what I was thinking the night before during the dinner. I told her who I was and what I do. I even shared my vision for the years to come. We laughed, entertained deep conversations, and even exchanged contacts to keep in touch. It was the perfect way to end the night and fly back home with enthusiasm.

When I returned home, I landed at JFK airport. I had to go through customs to get my luggage. The lines were long and a few people were coming back from the ceremony. Some had their posters and banners on hand from the ceremony. When it was my turn to have my passport stamped and asked questions, two security attendants at the booth greeted me. One was just there to observe while the other sat in the chair to ask me questions.

He asked me so many questions and kept looking at my passport. "You went to Norway?" I replied with a 'yes'. He asked my reason and I told him that it was for the Nobel Peace Prize Ceremony. Then, something that was unique to me started happening. His eyes began to water, and he started asking me questions about my experience. After I answered each question he would say, "Wow!" It didn't take long for the other security attendant to give his partner a look to end the conversation. So, he did and smiled at me while handing me back the passport. And right after I said, "Thank you," and began to walk, he said in a very calm and soft tone, "Brother, I am inspired and proud of you."

24

BECOMING
A SKYSCRAPER

When you know better, you do better. And when see more, your mind expands more. That is exactly what happened to me as time passed. I was no longer the homeless kid from Newark, New Jersey. I was no longer the dropout student trying to chase his big dream. I had become more and I was living out my biggest dreams. I was in documentaries that were featured in theatres, on primetime news, on front-page articles around the world. I was definitely living the dream.

Overtime, I learned how to meditate and incorporate ways to reflect and process my thoughts and ideas. That always was a way I could detach from the world to stay centered and hear God's voice. I had written a few books already that were keeping me busy. I noticed I wasn't impressed with them when I put them next to some of my favorite authors' books. They were okay but I wasn't impressed with taking them internationally with me.

One day, after my mindfulness meditation, I had an idea to write a book that would be high quality and would be able to impact the world. I didn't care about book sells or trying to become a best-selling author. I just wanted to write a book that would change someone's life. Period. I wanted it to have a powerful cover to let it known that I meant business. It would be the evolution of RahGor. I wanted the book to be read around the world and translated into many languages.

I began writing my notes and let my mind wander. I had a very large file of my random thoughts and wise words I'd collected over the years. I started going through them and reorganized all the papers so I could use them for my book. I started writing the book in Starbucks near my home every single day. I would arrive by 8 a.m. and write until the place closed down. It was pure dedication and discipline.

I eventually moved around to different places to write such as the library, Barnes & Noble café, local parks in New Jersey and New York. I eventually landed at a café in New York City called, Café Bene. It was an international café and people from all over the world visited, ordering with heavy accents. I loved every bit of it. They had a seating area in he back with books all around the walls and these cool light bulbs hanging from the ceiling. It was the perfect location for me to complete my book. It was there that I learned important lessons and met some of the coolest people from around the globe who would sit with me to push me to keep writing when I had writer's block or a brain freeze. I knew that this place would be where I would complete the last parts of my book.

Studying and Writing at Harvard

Prior to completing my book manuscript in New York City, I registered to study at Harvard University. They have a program called, Harvard Extension, where you take courses that you can apply toward getting a degree or certification. I wanted neither of these things because I wanted to just be a student. I wanted to perfect my craft as a speaker and speechwriter. I registered for an advance course in Business Executive

Speech with one of the top speech coaches and professors on the campus. I had no idea that deciding to begin a journey at Harvard would shift me in my writing, speaking, and the way I would think moving forward.

When I started my first day of class, I was still living in New Jersey. So, I had to wake up at 4:00 a.m. in the morning and head out to take a bus from Northern New Jersey into New York City. Then I would transfer to another bus from 34th street in Manhattan (NYC Time Square) that would take me to Boston, MA.

Once I arrived in Boston, I would have to take a train to Cambridge just so I could study and take my courses at Harvard every single week. Once I left class, I would take a train and bus to Medford, MA, where an amazing Jewish woman allowed me to stay overnight to rest before I headed back home the following day.

I never missed a class and never showed up late.

I did this every single week. Yes, every single week! I never missed a class and never showed up late. I was the first one there and the last one to leave. The traveling would be at least 5–6 hours. In all that I did, I still was able to become the top student in my class during that semester. I framed my first transcript like it was a degree.

Because of what I was trying to accomplish while at Harvard, my professor introduced me to a woman who became my speech coach and advisor. She had me meet with her for 90 minutes after my evening classes every week. I had more work than the rest of my fellow classmates because I was aiming for something more. To do something much more demanding and set myself on a path that had me walk alone more than often. This tends to happen when you yearn for something more than what you see around you.

I had been caught up in snowstorms. I was on campus during the horrible Boston Marathon bombing and experienced a city lockdown due to the manhunt. I was there debating, sharing my experiences, and laughing with like-minded humans when we would say, "Don't forget about me when you become president." My hunger to be great allowed me to experience moments that fulfilled me.

I would roam around campus to get inspired for my book and spent a great deal of time writing in the library and the law school. I spent winter nights in Harvard Square sipping hot chocolate and hearing the soundtrack from the movie, Social Network, about world renowned Facebook and Mark Zuckerburg. Sitting in my speech class, I came up with the opening of my book entitled, Role Models vs. Super Heroes.

After my semester completed, I said my goodbyes and knew what I experienced and learned would be the essential piece to finishing my book and launching a world tour once the book was complete.

The Skyscraper Book and World Tour

I completed the book shortly after my semester at Harvard. I spent the entire summer writing, editing, and restricting the manuscript. When it was completed, I felt a sense of accomplishment. I knew this book would seal the deal. I contacted my closest friends who were talented in certain areas and hired them to help me on the project. Once I had the complete version in my hand, I began planning the world tour.

Sold Out Seats to Hear RahGor Speak

I kicked off the tour in high fashion. I started off in Monterrey, Mexico and headed towards Europe next. I began seeing posters and banners at schools excited for my arrival. There were students and young leaders coming from everywhere. I made my way into Oslo, Norway and then Began, Norway. I made stops in Santiago, Chile and Gran Canaria. I flew to Porto, Portugal and then I had stops in Munich, Germany and Bavaria. I stopped in Austria and even found myself in Switzerland. What I had envisioned for my life truly changed my life. I became an international award-winning speaker.

RahGor Sells Out Carnegie Hall

The Skyscraper World Tour was running for 2 years strong. I began feeling the weight of traveling but I knew that to who much is given; much is required. So, I sucked it up and kept traveling and selling out shows all over the world. This sounds crazy writing all this; but, it is all facts.

Towards the middle of the second year, I knew I would have to take a break. I wanted to end it the way I started it. On top! I decided to achieve something that was beyond my normal: headlining a sold-out lecture at the world-renowned Carnegie Hall in New York City. And that's exactly what I did.

I want to share with you why this star aligning moment is something that many people miss in their lives. And I DO NOT want you to miss your star aligning moment. On September 21, 2017, I spoke to a sold out Carnegie Hall. Exactly two years prior to that date, September 21, 2015, I was at Carnegie Hall for the very first time attending an event to see a famous pianist. When I walked into the hall where the show was taking place, I was blown away by the beautiful space. How could I not take a picture from the back of the room to have as a keepsake? My girlfriend, at that specific time, just smiled and knew I was in my happy place. I watched as everyone came in dressed and excited. There were so many whispers and high energy just for being in the room. As we waited for the show, I showed her the picture and then it hit me. I immediately said to her, "What do you think of me having a lecture here? I don't think something like that has ever been done. What do you think?"

She said, "I think you should look into it. It would be awesome, Rah."

It was at that very moment, I knew I could do it. I could see it happening. I was obsessed with the idea, vision, and the emotions running through my entire body. When I got home, I spent some time going through the website, writing notes, and even sent out an email to the event coordinator before bed. The next day, I received the response with all the pricing and details needed to plan.

Note to Self:

- You MUST be obsessed with the vision to see it through.

- There will be many moving parts throughout the process of making it a reality so being obsessed can help you deal with whatever comes your way.

- See and get all the details together to master the process and make the moment one to remember.

Once I had all the details, I spent the next few days planning out the entire show. When all was completed from what I viewed on the paper, I reached out to the event coordinator to set the date. I was excited and thrilled until she said I would have to wait until January to see if the date would work. At that time, it was going into October and I wanted to lock in a date immediately! This is what happens when you are moving radically. Things will be on a high until you hit a red light moment. It is only then that your focus, willpower, and faith will begin to be tested. She said she would write down the date I wanted and get back to me in the beginning of the New Year. Keep in mind, I wanted a Wednesday in February of 2016.

So, 4 months go by. I had to continue to keep the vision alive and keep my enthusiasm up because even though there are no guarantees in life. I know that we MUST always choose to have RADICAL FAITH so what we envision will work out in our FAVOR.

January came along and nothing happened. No phone call or email. I got an email late in January to be made aware that they didn't finish completing their season calendar so they couldn't let me know when I would be able to get the date. I pushed the date back to late Aug/Sept. All I had to do was leave a deposit to secure the date. That wasn't possible at the time because I was preparing for tour and my funds were tied up in many things. I ended up telling her that I wasn't ready and I would try again next season.

A full year of keeping radical faith, radial thinking, radical action, and radical vision all while doing other impactful things. It took a lot out of me when I came to realize that the time was not aligned. When I spoke with the event coordinator, she was very understanding and stated to me that it would happen and she looked forward to keeping in touch for the following season.

It was a bit devastating because with all the blessings happening around me, I knew this vision was the radical test of my belief system and brilliance. How would I make this happen? This was the question EVERY SINGLE DAY. Then I decided to speak life constantly into my vision. I surrendered and focused on everything to be blessed and when the time was set, it would happen.

Fast forward another year later, it did happen. And it happened exactly on the date that I took the picture back on September 21, 2015. I was able to get a big enough contract to use part of the funding as a down payment on the venue and then spend almost 7 months to promote the event as the final stop on my global tour.

Everything was aligned and worked out as it was supposed to. People flew in from all over the world. My old high school honored me on the same month and then the school board sponsored two charter buses of students to attend the event. Montclair State University EOF program sponsored a group of students along with various programs and people that supported me over the years purchased tickets.

Then 2 weeks before the night, we announced that every seat in Carnegie Hall was completed sold out. It was a grand opening and closing to a major chapter in my life. Friends and family flew into New York from different countries, states, and cities. All I could do was walk on the stage and cry tears of joy. I really cried, too. I was crying so hard that when I tried to speak it sounded like gibberish. But I got through it and gave a speech to empower every person in the room. Then the unbelievable happened, when I gave my last line stating, "My Location Was Not My Destination" the crowd gave me a standing ovation. I bowed at the audience, looked at the crowd, and knew that I not only made it out, but I made my dreams come true.

25

THANK YOU
FOR READING

There were so many experiences that I wanted to share in my memoir, but I just wanted to share these specific experience with you because these moment always stuck with me. I believe they were the moments I had to make my most critical decision and lean on my faith wholeheartedly. We don't get the privilege to choose how or where we are born, but I believe we have the gift of choice on the paths we want to walk in life. Every path has detours and open roads at times. It won't always be easy but the feeling of walking a path that you chose can be extraordinary if we allow it to be.

You will have to surrender to a higher power greater than you. You will have to look deep within yourself to recognize that you will always be and have more than enough for the journey. You will have to acknowledge and understand the universal laws. You will need to understand that we do not fail but we do fall. As long as you are for sure that you will always get up, you will succeed in the most incredible way.

Your standards will change, so will your surroundings. Your conversations will change and so will the people you are around. Your focus will change and so will the views you will see. Your money will change and so will your habits. But believe me, fruitful is the life of those who walk their gardens to plant and water their seeds daily.

Thank you for reading my story.

Rahfeal was invited to give his Hip Hop Saved My Life Seminar
at a New Jersey high school.

Rahfeal reading letters from students late at night in his New York City office.

Rahfeal at a dinner celebration in Oslo, Norway to honor Malala Yousafzai the day before she received the Nobel Peace Prize.

Rahfeal speaking in Oslo, Norway at the Voices for World Peace event.

Rahfeal receives a standing ovation at Carnegie Hall after his lecture.

The promotional flyer for Hip Hop Saved My Life Seminar at New Jersey Performing Arts Center (NJPAC) in Newark, New Jersey.

Rahfeal at the Harvard Club in New York City in front of a
Reginald F. Lewis portrait.

26

THE STRATEGIES
FOR SOLUTIONS

The following are 23 strategies to help you find solutions if you are experiencing similar issues to what I went through in my life. As I share these strategies with you, please know that you MUST have unbreakable faith. You also must have an EXTREMELY diligent work ethic in order for these strategies to work for you. Let no one tell you that you can't get out of your situation (especially if he or she is in the same negative environment with you).

You were born to be great in your path. You were created to live, love, and laugh. Don't get me wrong; we all face storms in our lives, but there are rainbows afterwards. The individuals who see the rainbows are the ones who danced in the rain when others cried in the puddles.

STRATEGY

. . . .

I

Find mentors who are successful in your career area or the career area in which you desire to enter. Ask to spend fifteen minutes with them or have lunch with them once a month. When you have confirmed a mentor or mentors, ask questions and listen to their advice. These are the people who want to see you succeed and help remove you from your struggles.

STRATEGY

. . . .

2

Keep a journal to write or type your emotions. Writing is therapy that soothes the pain in your soul. When no one wants to hear you, vent on that paper or keyboard. Don't bottle up your feelings because it will hold you back. Think of a journal as a Band-Aid for a cut; it helps the healing.

STRATEGY

. . . .

3

Read books that have information to help you create the lifestyle you want (or remove you from a negative environment). These books are in categories that are titled "Self-Help." There are many books on numerous topics, but you should center on the books that build character, motivation, and focus on subjects that cater to what/who you want to become. If you want to be a doctor, read books from the medical field, but you should also read books that focus on personal development as well.

STRATEGY

. . . .

4

Find something for which you would die. This may seem like an extreme statement, but think about a person (could be you) who lives in an extremely negative environment where people are dying every day around them because of the evils of the street. You have to double your positive energy just to get through each day of living in that toxic situation. The goal is to have a POWERFUL "WHY". Why do you want to leave this toxic environment? Are the reasons so that you can live past 25, to start a family, and not have to worry about losing one of them before 18?

STRATEGY

. . . .

5

When your window of success is open, you must work harder, faster, and stronger because that window will not remain open forever. It will open and close at various times.

STRATEGY

· · · · · · · · · · · · · · · · ·

6

Become aware of what keeps you from taking the right steps and being resourceful. Then you must stop it.

STRATEGY

· · · · · · · · · · · · · · · · · · ·

7

There are many opportunities that will come your way, but you must understand that every opportunity isn't for you. When you have a clear focus on your mission, select the opportunities that will be beneficial to help accomplish it.

STRATEGY

· ·

8

Make quantum leaps in your life. To do this, you will have to visualize yourself as already being successful. In other words, pretend you have already achieved your goal. You need to become that person on the inside, and then you will attract success into your life. The reason why visualization works is that the unconscious mind cannot tell the difference between what is real and what is imagined. So if you imagine something, your mind makes it real and brings it to reality.

STRATEGY

9

Spend at least ten minutes in front of the mirror every morning describing who you are for the day. Examples: I am amazing; I am a great business person; I am an honor roll student; I am going to be a college student; I am the best father/mother for my children.

STRATEGY

· · · · · · · · · · · · · · · · · · · ·

10

Take trips to the areas where you want to live. If you remain in an environment that you don't enjoy for a long time, you can be in a depressed state of mind. It is best to visit environments that make you happy, relieves stress, or where you can imagine living.

STRATEGY

Slowly remove fear, anger, shame, and guilt because they are forms of toxic emotions that cloud your ability to perceive the truth. This hurts relationships because when you have these emotions, a person you may need in your life will not be open with you.

STRATEGY

· ·

12

Intensify what you can do and find individuals who can intensify what you can't.

STRATEGY

· · · · · · · · · · · · · · · · · · · ·

13

Plan an exit strategy. Research and plan before you make major moves. If you take the time to do both of these things, you will get out of anything and won't have to worry about going back.

STRATEGY

. . . .

14

Don't tell everyone your plans because you may have many crabs around you, and they will want to keep you down with them. Just work hard and smart! Don't worry about what others are doing. You have to get out of where you are.

STRATEGY

. . . .

15

Find programs that can help you get the things you don't have. These programs can focus on getting a college degree, high school diploma, a trip out of the country, insight on how to start a business, or how to be the best at a particular activity. No matter what the focus may be, make sure you find as many programs and resources as possible.

STRATEGY

· · · · · · · · · · · · · · · · · · ·

16

If your inner circle is not challenging, you will have to change the people inside. You MUST stay among those who will challenge you and inspire you to live better.

STRATEGY

. . . .

17

Act as if you are already where you want to be. The mind will attract all the things to you that you think you are. Always remember you are what you think. Don't think negatively because the mind will connect you to all negativity and keep you in a negative environment.

STRATEGY

18

Challenge and make goals for yourself. It is very important that you set goals that excite you but at the same time make you work hard to build what you never had.

STRATEGY

19

Create a vision board. Take a poster board and paste pictures and words that define your future and who you plan to be. Keep this in a place that you will see it every single day. Use magazines and old books to cut out these pictures. This vision board is to help you see the future!

STRATEGY

· · · · · · · · · · · · · · · · · · · ·

20

Think about the worst that could happen before you make a decision. You may have already started making changes in your life, so you have multiple opportunities coming your way. Remember that every opportunity that comes your way isn't always good for you. Think things through and then make a decision. If you have to make an emotional decision, us your gut as it will never steer you wrong.

STRATEGY

. . . .

21

Read daily positive affirmations and articles that are inspirational. These readings will help trigger innovative ideas to make your life more positive.

STRATEGY

22

Ask for help when needed. Do not have too much pride to ask for help when struggling. You will get to the promise land, but you can't get there all by yourself. You need assistance and guidance. Those willing to help you get there are the ones you should treasure like gold.

STRATEGY

. . . .

23

When things get really dark and it seems that there will be no light, say, "My location is not my destination." Repeat it over and over again until you are balanced and have a grip on yourself. It is a MUST to give yourself self-motivation because there will be times in your life when no one will be around. It will only be you and the thoughts in your head. However, you will get through because you are special, and you already know this. Embrace the struggle, and it will take you to personal freedom.

27

RAHGOR
DAILY AFFIRMATIONS

Directions: Say one affirmation twice each day. Once in the morning and once before you go to bed. You MUST say these affirmations to yourself in the mirror with confidence. After each one, say, "I can and I will." This will help you get in a positive state of mind to make daily personal changes. Be good. Live prosperous.

DAY

· · · · · · · · · · · ·

1

Today, I embrace change in my life.
As I continue to grow and blossom in the field
of life, I will be the reflection of beauty. Today, I
spread the purest love I hold within. Today, I move
mountains, split seas, and align the stars within my
universe to receive all that I envision.

DAY

· · · · · · · · · · · ·

2

Today will be AMAZING. I will command the attention of every eye in the room because of the godly spirit that is within me. I will smile more today than I did yesterday. I will say thank you more because today I receive more. Today my lifestyle has more value and my life has more meaning!

DAY
. . . .
3

Today, I attract WEALTH and PROSPERITY. I am money magnetic, and all forms of prosperity look for me. Today, I CLAIM valuable gifts, job bonuses, checks in the mail, increases in savings accounts, and amazing increased percentages on the stocks in which I have invested. I SPEAK PROSPERITY over my life today, and all those who are attached to me will prosper. Today, I become increasingly rich in financial numbers and wealthy in financial intelligence.

DAY

. . . .

4

There is no one I would rather be than I! I claim greatness and all the deepest forms of love to be within my life. Today, the world will show me love, and I will show it back double time. I am more than average today. I am the complete form of amazement and beauty.

DAY

. . . .

5

Today, I am completely FREE and the creator of my destiny. For the next 10 years, I will defy the laws of gravity and not give into the "chicken mentality" of the world. Today, I am an EAGLE that knows it was created to fly high! Today, I see my omens and thank the heavens for what they have and will be sending me!

DAY

. . . .

6

Today, I walk my dreams down the aisle to marry them. I am changing their last names from (say your first name) dreams to (say your first name) goals. Today, I plan to accomplish and enjoy them with the little time I have on this earth. Today, I marry my visions, my passions, my desires, and my true happiness.

DAY

· · · · · · · · · · · · ·

7

Today, I CLAIM THE EXTRAORDINARY! I claim that new car! I claim that new home! I claim having the children I always wanted! I claim that wife/husband! I claim joy, happiness, peace, positive energy, and love! I claim that college degree! I claim that job position! I claim a better life than the one I have now! I claim what will make me happy because I was not born to struggle nor be unhappy in this AMAZING LIFE! Today, I claim and change for the better.

DAY

. . . .

8

Today, I plant the seeds of forever. I will leave my mark on the hearts of family, friends, and strangers. Today, I will show the next generation how to survive when they become the old generation. I will enjoy this moment so that when it becomes the past, I can enjoy it as a memory in the future. Today, I will be what I will be remembered for when I am no longer here.

DAY

. . . .

9

On this day, life has given me diamonds and pearls to share with all those who are around me. I feel so blessed to be given complete access to the treasures of the world. Today, I walk with intense faith as I move forward into the unknown hours of today. I may not know what the total day will bring, but I do know that I bring gifts of love, peace, joy, style, and enthusiasm. Today, I am wealthy in mind, body, and soul!

DAY

· · · · · · · · · · · ·

10

Today, I am stepping out on my faith. I cannot be scared if I am excited for what I am pursuing. I am on this earth for a certain mission and one purpose. Today, I move closer to my purpose by completing my missions. I am far from where I came, and that means I can DO THIS! Today is here, and today I have NO FEAR!

DAY

11

Today, I smile because I lost count of all the many blessings I have received in my life. Even though I am flawed, I have so many people who accept me for who I am. Today, I celebrate with smiles and positive gestures. Today, I give kisses, handshakes, hugs, eye winks, and text messages that end with a smiley face. Today, I am just thankful for my life.

DAY

. . . .

12

Today, I love myself just the way I am. I know that there are BILLIONS of people in the world, but there is no one like me. Today, I laugh more, smile more, hug more, kiss more, and dance more. I will make this day feel like the LOVE I want to experience every day. I am who I am, and those who accept me for who I am will know who I am.

DAY

·····················

13

Today, I will focus on being a better person than I was yesterday. I forgive those who left me, hurt me, lied to me, and neglected me. I am MORE than what others believe I am. Today, I will capture the love that is created in moments. I will smile at happiness and hug joyful situations. I, (say name), am grateful for all I have experienced, and I am looking forward to being a great experience to someone else.

DAY

· · · · · · · · · · · ·

14

Yesterday is where I will leave all my troubles. In yesterday, I prayed for a day of change, and that day is TODAY. I claim that my storm is over! Today, I turn my wrongs into rights. I leave behind unhealthy relationships, harmful eating habits, imperfections, negativity, darkness, and immaturity in the days of YESTERDAY. I embrace love, positivism, God, balance, light, new relationships, and the smiles of my guardian angels.

DAY

· · · · · · · · · · · ·

15

Today, I have ENORMOUS faith! I am
moving the TALLEST mountain and moon walking
across the WIDEST ocean in my life. Today, I am
equipped with the tools to FIX the problems and
build the foundations needed in my life. Today, I
SPEAK into the world the things I want to see and
who I want to be.

DAY

16

Today, I know better so I will do better! What I believe will be conceived and received. Today, I think twice but will speak once. My seeds of yesterday are sprouting today! So I will continue to water it with pure love, powerful thoughts, positive words, and positive energy!

DAY

. . . .

17

Today, I receive all within the all.

I will send out positive compliments to all those I know because a compliment is another glue that holds relationships together. Today, I intensify my love and passion towards life. This day has arrived, and TODAY, I will do nothing but be thankful to be ALIVE!

DAY

18

I am just the most amazing and unique person on the planet. I control my emotions and thoughts today. I am climbing mountains and breaking down walls in my life with ease. Today is my life without any boundaries!

DAY

. . . .

19

Today, my dreams flirt with my reality. I will allow myself to enjoy the true intimacy of life. Today is sexy because I am sexy. I will be more tempting to those who lay eyes on me because my spirit is attractive. Today, I walk on water as I allow my life to put on a fashion show for all those who meet me today.

DAY

. . . .

20

Today will be simply beautiful. My positive thoughts and blessings will flow like the Nile River into my garden of life. I will glow brighter so that my kids, friends, and family members will always have a light to see. Today, I will be all I can be within all that I see and surround me. Today is simply beautiful because I am.

DAY

. . . .

21

Today, God dwells within me as me.
I will allow my light to shine from the highest
mountain upon the cities (people). Today, I am
radiant and simply powerful. Today, I leave alone
the scabs of the past so that my healing process
can completely pass.

DAY

22

Today has nothing to do with what has already happened. Today is the exact seed I need so that I can grow tomorrow. I will be open for financial gain and wisdom today. I will be who I want to be today so that I will not have regret tomorrow. Today, I claim great health, wealth, and prosperity in my life!

DAY

23

Today, I am just amazed at how fine, beautiful, handsome, sexy, and radiant I am! Today, I will think BIG and smile BIG. Today, I will walk like a king/queen because my life was crowned with GREATNESS. I will get rid of those who are toxic and think like peasants. I cannot waste my time that is just as valuable as rubies and gold! Today, my life is BLAZING and AMAZING!

DAY

24

Today, I claim QUANTUM LEAPS in my life. I move forward with a peace of mind. I will receive so many blessings today that my mouth will hurt from saying THANK YOU. I will be the light for the children who are in darkness, and I will be the smile that my family and friends need today. I am sexy, I am wonderful, and I am God's beautiful masterpiece!

DAY

25

Today, I embrace change in my life. As I continue to grow and blossom in the field of life, I will be the reflection of beauty. Today, I preserve my sexiness while spreading the purest love I hold within. Today, I move mountains, split seas, and align the stars within my universe to receive all that I envision!

DAY

· · · · · · · · · · · ·

26

Today will be AMAZING. I will command the attention of every eye in the room because of the godly spirit that is within me. I will smile more today than I did yesterday. I will say thank you more because today I receive more. Today, my lifestyle has more value, and my life has more meaning!

DAY

. . . .

27

Today was created with doors to wealth and opportunities. Today, I will walk into any room and illuminate it with my spirit. I am more handsome, sexy, brilliant, amazing, and determined than I was yesterday. Today, I will let nothing hold me back because I am great, and great people only move forward!

DAY

28

Today, I claim QUANTUM LEAPS in my life. Today will be better than it was yesterday. I will allow wealth, love, healthy relationships, blessings, and happiness to enter my life today. Today, I turn impossible into I'M POSSIBLE!

DAY

. . . .

29

Today, I will be able to unlock the doors to my new life. I have packed up all my old issues and shipped them to God's hands. Today, I will be shopping for new things to make my house (life) as comfortable as it can be. Today, I am excited for the new memories I will be creating within my life. I am excited for all those who will enter my life to enjoy the house warming. Today, I close and become the owner of the house I always wanted.

DAY

. . . .

30

Today, the secrets of life will be revealed to me. I am becoming wealthier in mind, body, and soul. Today, the secrets to success will be told to me. The more I seek for success, the more it will show itself to me. Today, my life is the complete example of Laws of Attraction.

The words I speak today will become my reality. The words I speak today will manifest right in front of my eyes. Today, I will speak things into existence with my gift of words. I speak prosperity today! I speak great health today! I speak achievement today! I speak a career promotion today! I speak life into the world of those who lost their souls! I speak happiness within my family today! I speak longevity and legacy over my life today! Today, I speak blessings into the world!

CPSIA information can be obtained
at www.ICGtesting.com
Printed in the USA
BVHW092304250822
645539BV00005B/15

9 781734 631678